2012

# The Sharecropper's Daughter

*Clara Petty*

authorHOUSE®

*AuthorHouse™*
*1663 Liberty Drive*
*Bloomington, IN 47403*
*www.authorhouse.com*
*Phone: 1-800-839-8640*

*First published by AuthorHouse 10/28/2010*

*ISBN: 978-1-4520-7038-4 (sc)*

*Printed in the United States of America*

*This book is printed on acid-free paper.*

*For Douglas and Scott*

# Acknowledgments

Thanks to my forever friend, Bonnie, without whose help this book would not have been possible; my friend Lou, who provided valuable assistance; and God, for giving me the courage to write this book. The people and events described in this book reflect the author's actual experiences. Some names have been changed to protect the privacy of certain individuals and their families.

*Chapter 1*

♣

*Family*

I was born in rural St. Francis County, Arkansas, the third of five children born into the Adkins Family. The oldest was Bill, followed by four girls: —Maxine, me, Marilyn, and Glenda. All the girls were, over time, bestowed with nicknames that stuck till we were grown. Maxine was Mac. I was Tootsie—Tootie or Toots for short. Marilyn and one of Daddy's dogs shared the nickname Deak. Glenda, whose middle name is Ruth, became Baby Ruth.

Glenda entered the world on a clear moonlit night in August 1944. She was the last child born to my parents and the only one of their five to be born in a hospital or clinic. At five years old, I had no idea my mother was even pregnant; we never discussed such personal issues in our household. The night Glenda arrived, Mama moaned, and I got up to see her dressed and brushing her hair. I asked, "What's wrong?" and she said she was "having spells." She couldn't bring herself to say "labor pains."

When Mama and Daddy left for the hospital, Daddy said to my twelve-year-old brother, Bill: "Stay at the house till daylight, and then you and the other kids go to your Uncle Elbert's house."

No sooner were our parents out of sight than Bill got Daddy's hunting cap and, as he had seen Daddy do many times, attached a carbide light to the cap's bill. "Get dressed," he said, and we took off on the mile-long walk through the woods in the middle of the night. Bill led the way by use of the carbide light while carrying two-year-old Marilyn, with Maxine and me following.

I still get goose bumps remembering that dangerous

trek through the dark woods at night—in an area with a reputation of being rife with rattlesnakes. Surprisingly, when Daddy found out about our midnight walk, he wasn't upset—maybe he was even a little proud of his son for having the courage to lead us like that, though he never told Bill so.

❧

Maxine and Marilyn were the family beauties. With their lush, dark, wavy hair, beautiful eyes, and symmetrically arranged features, they attracted more than their share of boyfriends and attention from family and well-meaning friends. Despite her china-doll features, Marilyn was a tomboy and could hold her own with the neighborhood boys. Knowing I had an aversion to frogs, she delighted in chasing me with fat toads clutched in her hand as I ran screaming as though my life depended on putting distance between us.

Glenda, the youngest sister, was a cute, cuddly kid known for her impulsiveness. More than once, she chopped off her long, dreamy eyelashes with scissors because they bothered her by raking her eyebrows. She would sit in Mama's lap and scream from the pain of the cut-off lashes sticking into her eyes as the lashes grew back.

As for me, I thought of myself as "the plain one"—the tall, skinny middle child with stringy, board-straight hair. When relatives and friends came to visit, their attention was usually focused on Maxine and Marilyn and the guys they were presently dating. Being sandwiched between them in birth order made it hard, especially since Mama's attention often centered around them and their boyfriends also.

Growing up feeling awkward, I suffered from a lack of self-confidence which lasted until I became self-sufficient and gained acceptance in the adult world. Maintaining a quiet demeanor, I accepted what life had to offer but always with an eye toward a better future. I felt it was up to me to make my own success, and by applying God-given determination and wisdom, I hoped to get what I wanted out of life.

My mother was a lovely, gentle woman whose greatest joy was caring for her family. Best known for her generous, kind, and caring spirit, she demonstrated daily the meaning of sacrifice, patience, and love. Her oft-repeated mottos were: *Treat others as you would like to be treated* and *Always look for the good in everyone.* Even now, I find it surprising how much of my life has been defined by her—no matter how far away I got—and how much remained the same after she was gone.

One of my earliest memories is of sitting on the floor listening to the thump-thump of Mama pedaling the treadle of her sewing machine. Not an expert seamstress, she sewed out of necessity. She made everything from dresses to quilts, and as she sewed, she prayed for her family. Knowing Mama, that meant a lot of tears were mixed among the stitches.

After the death of her brother's young wife, Mama welcomed him and any number of his children into our home at any time. It didn't matter that they often showed up at awkward family times or even unannounced during meals. She just put on another skillet of potatoes and mixed up another batch of cornbread to go with the big pot of beans on the stove. Mama always managed and never complained.

Mama had grown up on a farm, along with her sister and two brothers. Her father, Lee Webb, was a highly intelligent man. People traveled miles to seek his knowledge on business matters, such as filing taxes, buying and selling property, and interpreting complicated government forms. Despite having only an eighth grade education, he taught school in the local community where he raised his family. My middle name is Lee, and I am proud to be his namesake.

Shortly before the 1929 stock market crash, my grandfather moved his family from St. Francis County, Arkansas, to the town of Black Rock. Having made a good cotton crop in St. Francis County that year and being assured it had been sold at a good price, he built a nice two-story house in Black Rock.

However, when time came for Granddaddy to receive the income from his cotton, he found the cotton hadn't been sold until after the market crashed. Receiving only a fraction of what his cotton had been worth at the higher price, he was forced to give up the new home and return to St. Francis County to start over.

Daddy, unfortunately, had few of Mama's attributes. Though he loved his family and worked hard to provide for us, his violent temper and extreme mood swings were fearful. He would surely be diagnosed in today's world as a classic bipolar case, at best. Though soft-spoken, my mother was not afraid to stand up to him, and there were often fierce arguments and physical confrontations between them.

I lived in constant anxiety due to Daddy's moods. The slightest things sent him into towering rages. Worse, you never knew when to expect Daddy's violent mood swings, which seemed to be triggered by nothing. I often woke up to him screaming, cursing, and acting like an enraged bull. Our screen doors sometimes had to be replaced due to his kicking them open.

Although we didn't have running water, Daddy expected a kettle of hot water to be available at all times. I can still hear the sound of the kettle being slammed on the top of the stove when he found it empty. The same went for the water bucket that provided our drinking water, which was drawn from the cistern.

Many nights I lay awake, trembling while listening to Daddy rant and rave, swearing and cursing over nothing in particular—just everyday living. Fear and hope were the guideposts in my life: fear that Daddy's temper would explode into violence and hope that someday things would get better. I was thankful we didn't have neighbors living close enough to hear his frequent outbursts.

I promised myself that my children would never be exposed to such turmoil. I never felt my parents realized the harm this does to a child. Daddy was capable of physical violence, and I feared for my mother. She tried to explain the bruises she received from his physical abuse with the classic excuses about "having fallen down the back steps." I grew up feeling helpless—helpless to help Mama and helpless to stop their fighting. As I became older, I withdrew into myself, developing a love of reading as a means of escape.

For Mama, leaving Daddy was not an option. With five children and little education, she was an economic slave with nowhere to go. Besides, in spite of my father's tirades and ill treatment of her, she loved him.

Later in life, as I struggled to understand why Daddy always seemed angry, I came to the realization that the responsibilities of raising a large family just as the country was climbing out of a deep depression probably contributed to his resentment and tremendous frustration. Constantly worried about whether his family of seven could reap enough to get by, he had the incredible task of planning and organizing the means required to survive with very limited resources and supplies.

Mama never let Daddy physically discipline us; she feared he couldn't control his temper. She was passive and sweet-natured, but when it came to her children, she could

7

be a lioness. She did not waver in protecting us from his tantrums and rages.

Once when Daddy was raging and threatening to beat up one of my sisters because she had left on a date with someone he didn't approve of, Mama quietly met my sister at the front door when she returned and saw her safely to bed. Actually, my brother, sisters, and I had a reputation for being so well behaved that discipline was rarely an issue. Our motivation was fear.

Despite Daddy's fearsome rule and hot temper, he displayed a strong protective side if he felt his family to be in danger. One day as Daddy was at the barn working on his old Model A Ford, he saw a rabid dog heading toward our house. My sisters and I were playing in the front yard under a big oak tree when we saw Daddy running toward us as fast as he could, waving his arms and shouting something.

We couldn't hear what he was saying but knew we needed to do something, so we ran toward the main gravel road. When we got to the road, we saw we had run straight toward a large dog with a swollen tongue hanging out of his mouth. It was then we realized Daddy had been yelling for us to get inside the house, but we had run the wrong way. Fortunately, Daddy got there just in time to keep us from being attacked by the rabid dog.

❧

In the early 1940s, we lived in a three-room house with no electricity, no running water, and no inside bathroom. During the winter, heat came from a pot-bellied wood-burning stove in the living room. Quilts were piled high on the beds for warmth at night since there was no heat in the bedrooms. In the early years, my parents and the five of us children all slept in one room. My brother Bill, sleeping on a roll-away bed, was once bitten by a rat!

Since we had no electricity, light was provided by kerosene lamps. One of our chores was to fill the lamps with kerosene in the mornings so we didn't have to do it at night in the darkness. We were one of the few families in the area who possessed a fancy Aladdin kerosene lamp.

Sitting at the table doing homework and reading by the Aladdin lamp was a big improvement over peering through the flickering light of a flat-wick kerosene lamp. Aladdin lamps used a round wick, which provided an even, unflickering flame and produced a great deal more light. The difference between the light of the Aladdin and any other lamp was so great that the company offered a thousand-dollar reward to anyone who could show them an oil lamp that could produce as much light. To our knowledge no one ever collected the reward.

The cistern, which supplied water for the family, consisted of a round concrete structure jutting about four feet above the ground and extending about thirty to forty feet beneath the earth. Stones or concrete lined the bottom. A trough attached to the roof of the house was slanted to collect rainwater and direct it into the cistern. An overhead pulley held a rope attached to a water bucket. The bucket was lowered into the cistern, allowed to fill with water, and then brought to the surface using a pulley, which made it much easier to haul the heavy bucket back up.

༄

In 1949 we moved from the flat bottomland into a house in the hills on Crowley's Ridge in the New Castle community. New Castle consisted of a general store, a cotton gin, and a church. The community population was only around one hundred people, but I have many fond memories of the people who lived, worked, and attended church in that little community.

Not only did the New Castle house have four rooms for the seven of us instead of three rooms, we also had electricity. We still had an outdoor toilet, drew water from a cistern, and heated our home with firewood, but the move was definitely a step up.

Other than having an extra bedroom and electricity, the house itself was not much of an improvement: no insulation, floors covered with cheap linoleum rugs laid over rough wood planks, and wallpaper used as much to cover the cracks in the walls as to cover the ugly exposed boards.

Daily visits to the outhouse in the cold of winter encouraged us to make our exits as quickly as possible. Not only was there no heat in the toilet, but it left our backsides exposed to the elements.

The New Castle house had a kitchen, living room, and two bedrooms. One bedroom held two full-size beds and a chest; the second room was just large enough for a bed and dresser but only if you turned sideways to get between the bed and dresser.

One of the top dresser drawers in the tiny bedroom held interesting things—stuff to show the neighborhood kids or cousins—like a long rattler taken from a rattlesnake Daddy had killed. The snakes get new rattle segments each time they shed their skin, and the snakes shed several times a year. Based on the length of the rattler, we deduced that one must have been a whopper.

One slow summer day, as I was poring over the contents of one of those dresser drawers, I found a bone. Thinking it was from a wild animal Daddy had killed, I showed it to Mama. "Shouldn't this be thrown away?" I asked. "Put that back where you found it," Mama said. "That is from your daddy's ribcage." It turned out to be one of Daddy's rib bones, which had been removed during surgery.

I didn't understand the importance of keeping the bone but did as she said. Mama went on to explain, "While your Daddy was jacking up a large truck, the jack slipped and hit him, breaking his jaw, and the truck fell on him. He was hospitalized for months, with his life in jeopardy, and he developed pneumonia and required further surgery." Although he eventually recovered, he was never as strong as he had been before the accident.

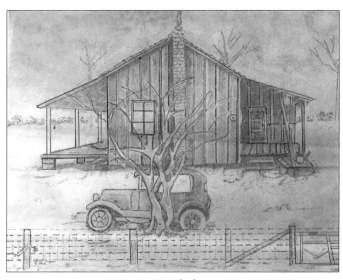

**New Castle house**

*Chapter 2*

♣

*The Cotton Patch*

Long before the mechanization of cotton picking equipment, I already had a strong incentive to strive for better things. It was called the cotton patch.

Cotton farming was vital to the inhabitants of rural areas in the South in the 1940s and 1950s. Daddy owned no land. He did his best to eke out a living as a tenant farmer. We had no money coming in during the spring and summer months and lived off a furnish. A *furnish* consisted of a few dollars a month and credit at Horton's Grocery Store. The grocery bill and furnish were paid off in the fall when the cotton was harvested. What, if anything, was left over carried us through the winter.

There were two types of tenant farmers: share tenants and sharecroppers. The tenant farmer rented land and a house from a farm owner and then cultivated with his own seed and farming equipment, making use of his family's labor. A sharecropper was a resident laborer who was given a house by the owner and received monthly cash advances to tide the family over until the end of the season. The only farmers who made money owned their own land. The renters just tried to break even each year. Sharecroppers, like us, had it worst of all with little hope of ever getting ahead.

I had barely turned nine years old when I began working in the cotton fields. A skinny kid at less than fifty pounds, I chopped and picked cotton from early morning till almost dark, taking about an hour's break for lunch. That summer of 1948, our only mode of transportation, an old Model A Ford, quit running. Since one of our larger cotton fields sat about a mile from our house, Daddy, Bill, Maxine, and I walked to the field, chopped cotton all morning, walked back to the house for lunch, walked back to the field afterward, and again walked home near dark after finishing for the day.

Until I was ten years old, we farmed land at the base of Crowley's Ridge in St. Francis County. The flat Delta terrain contained a kind of soil called gumbo. Gumbo was especially hard to cultivate because it stuck together in clods. As I attempted to chop the weeds, grass, and vines from around the cotton stalks, my hoe, hitting the rock-hard-dirt clods, made ringing noises.

On the first chopping in May and June, the cotton choppers thinned the cotton plants and removed any weeds or grass that had come up along with the cotton. During planting, the tractor-pulled cotton planter placed more seed in the rows than was needed to assure a good stand of cotton. Thinning with a hoe eliminated extra plants and prevented overcrowding. Daddy taught us to leave a space one-and-a-half times the length of the metal hoe blade between each "hill" of cotton and to leave two plants in each hill to grow to maturity.

By the time we finished the first chopping, it was usually time for the second chopping. During the second chopping, the cotton choppers removed grass and weeds that had come up in the rows and between the cotton stalks since the first chopping.

My father, a perfectionist, thrived on praise from neighbors who took notice of his clean cotton fields. The majority of farmers chopped their cotton twice each summer, but we always chopped ours three times. We had the cleanest fields around—no grass, no weeds.

Though the cotton was plowed periodically, many types of weeds and grass had to be chopped by hand from the cotton rows: crabgrass, nut grass, and Johnson grass—the hated Johnson grass! Daddy insisted we dig it up by the roots, otherwise the Johnson grass would spring back in just a few days, taller than ever. A tough vine we called "cow-H vines" was especially hard to chop. I later learned the proper name for this vine was trumpet creeper; it was nicknamed "cow-itch" because it made cows itch. As was common in rural areas, *cow-itch* eventually became *cow-H*.

Only two pieces of equipment were needed for chopping cotton: a hoe and a long metal file to keep the blade of the hoe sharp. Hearing Daddy file the hoes each morning signaled it was almost time to go to the field. The file made a distinct grinding sound as it cut into the soft metal of the hoe. How I hated that sound! We always went home to eat lunch, and the sound of hoes being filed let us know our lunch break was about over and it was time to load up in the back of the pickup truck and head back to the field.

Cotton chopping was hot, backbreaking work. Stifling heat rose from the ground by midmorning. Ninety- to 100-degree temperatures in the open air rose to 110 or 120 degrees in the fields. I often searched for even just one cloud in the sky to shade the sun. Sweat rolled down my body and evaporated in the dry heat. At times I saw heat waves simmering across the tops of the cotton plants like ocean waves.

Even though on most days the temperature climbed to over one hundred degrees, we always wore long pants, long-sleeve shirts, and straw hats to protect us from long hours in the boiling sun. Cotton gloves kept our hands from blistering from the constant movement of the hoe handles; but even with gloves, calluses formed on the palms of our hands and stayed there for years after we had left the farm.

We made rounds, chopping to the end of one row and then turning around and chopping another row to get back to the water jug under the shade tree. Daddy wrapped a wet burlap bag around the glass gallon jug to keep it cool for as long as possible. But by morning or afternoon's end, the water had warmed. We passed the warm jug around, and all drank from it. Fear of being exposed to germs was far down the list of concerns when working in the fields.

If there existed a positive side to chopping and picking cotton, it was seeing the change in Daddy's demeanor as we all worked together in the field. He seemed a different person from the man at home—much calmer and kinder. When exhaustion set in toward the end of the day and I was lagging behind the others, he rushed to finish chopping or picking his row of cotton so he could turn around and help me get to the end of my row. We then got a few minutes rest before starting another row.

If we got through chopping our cotton early enough during the season, we hired out and chopped for others at three dollars a day. This was even harder than working in our own fields. We had the same long hours, but there was no rest at the end of each row.

❧

Late August or early September signaled the beginning of cotton picking season. Before invention of the cotton picking machine, all cotton was picked by hand, which meant picking each opened boll individually. Before farmers began chemically treating cotton to stunt its growth and allow the cotton picking machines to work properly, cotton grew taller than it does today. Cotton stalks averaged waist-high, but the "rank" cotton, which grew in low damp areas, would often grow five or six feet tall far above our heads.

❧

There were two positions assumed in picking cotton. Though the plants were sometimes taller than me, many of the bolls hung close to the ground, requiring me to stoop or bend to pick the cotton from the bolls and put them in my cotton sack. Or when bending over for long periods became too painful for my back, I crawled on my knees. Kneeling, of course, was painful too, especially on my bony knees.

Leather kneepads were available, but since we couldn't afford them, I sometimes made my own from an old cotton sack.

The cotton sack was a long, tan-colored canvas sack with a wide strap of the same rough material. The strap hung over my shoulder, adjusted by knots so the opening was easy to reach. The better cotton sacks had tar bottoms that helped us pull the sacks smoothly along the cotton rows. As the sack started to fill, cotton accumulated near the opening, so we would have to stop and shake it down to the bottom of the sack.

As the sack filled, it became heavier to drag. When the weight became too much and the sack began cutting into our shoulders, we carried it to the wagon or cotton trailer. Each sack was weighed before it was emptied into the wagon. This gave Daddy a good idea of how much cotton had been picked so he would know when he had a bale.

The cotton scale, usually affixed to the back of the cotton wagon, consisted of a long iron scale hanging from the wagon by a hook and a weight called a "pea," which was used to determine the correct amount of cotton in the sack. In order to hang the cotton sack on the weighing scales, it was customary to put a green cotton boll or a small rock inside the corner of the sack, and twist a wire around the boll and sack to make an oval wire loop by which to hang the sack.

As a child, I could pick around 100 pounds of cotton a day. As I grew older, I would average between 150 and 200 pounds, though I never quite reached 200. One day I was determined to pick 200, but the most I could get was 196 pounds. As I picked cotton in Uncle Elbert's field that day, he could see how hard I was working. When I came up 4 pounds short of 200, he said he would just give me the 4 pounds and put it down as 200. I appreciated it, but it wasn't the same as doing it on my own.

The wagon was taken to the gin when enough cotton had been picked to make a bale. A full bale of cotton usually consisted of about 1,400 pounds of cotton. Getting a chance to ride in the full wagon or trailer to Horton's cotton gin was a rare treat. As I sat atop the cotton piled high up the sides of the tall wagon, I liked to pretend I was riding on a cloud.

The cotton gin and the adjacent country store were exciting places to be during the fall season; there was lots of activity among the farmers. Bales of cotton were lined up in an endless row waiting to be ginned. Horton's Store, located next to the gin, was a convenient place to get an occasional soda pop or candy bar.

Sometimes when Daddy had gotten a small check at the gin for his cottonseed, he would stop on the way home from the field and buy a loaf of bread and a pound of bologna for supper. This was a treat, especially for Mama since she had picked cotton all afternoon and wouldn't have to cook supper after we got home from the field.

**Horton's Store**

**Horton's cotton gin**

Daddy sometimes hired black or white "hands," which is what people called anyone who helped someone else harvest their crop for pay. If the cotton bolls opened at about the same time, it was important to have the first picking done before fall rains set in. Rain could cause the cotton to fall out of the bolls prematurely and become discolored, thereby decreasing the price when it was ready to sell. We picked cotton alongside the black hands and often heard them singing church hymns and old spirituals. "Go Down Moses" was a particular favorite of mine.

Occasionally, some neighbor kids showed up on Saturday and asked to pick cotton to make a little extra money. We could tell how inexperienced they were by how they approached the job. If they were new to picking cotton, we smiled as they started picking with one hand, showing how green they were. Picking cotton required two hands simultaneously gathering the fluffy white cotton out of the bolls.

Picking cotton was no easier than chopping, but the cooler fall temperatures made it a little less miserable. I can still see Daddy and Mama and us kids moving slowly down the cotton rows with cotton sacks strapped over our shoulders, picking cotton, often pricking our fingers on the sharp burrs that held the cotton inside each boll. Our fingers often bled from being stabbed by the sharp ends of the burrs. On cold days our fingers turned blue from the early morning frost on the cotton bolls.

Federal child labor laws in the United States, created to protect children under the age of eighteen who work, don't apply to children working on farms owned or operated by a parent. There is no limit to how early in the day a child may begin work or how late they may work, nor is there a limit on the number of hours they can work during the day. Legally, children on farms are permitted to work at age twelve—and even younger.

Federal and state agricultural labor laws are less restrictive than those applied to other industries. The minimum age for children who work in fast food restaurants and department stores is fourteen years, and in those jobs, they can't work more than three hours a day or more than eighteen hours a week when school is in session; nor can they work more than eight hours a day or more than forty hours a week when school is not in session.

Despite agriculture's ranking as one of the three most dangerous industries in the United States, the law permits children to begin working on farms at a younger age and for longer hours than other working youth. In 2007 a bill called the Children's Act for Responsible Employment (CARE) was introduced to curb unfair child labor practices in agriculture that allow young children to work in dangerous conditions. However, as in other federal child labor laws, the bill preserves the family farm exemption that enables children of any age to continue to work on their parents' farms.

In any given week, thousands of children in the United States—many as young as eight years old—labor as I did, up to fifty or sixty hours a week. Federal laws permit children twelve and younger to work in extreme heat doing farm work but don't permit those same children to work in air-conditioned offices.

The laws and enforcement practices of individual states are no better than the federal laws and are sometimes worse. Many states don't even have minimum age requirements for children working in agriculture.

Young farm workers have a school dropout rate of between 50 to 65 percent. The notion that oppressive child labor occurs illegally within the United States shocks educators and the general public as well. In an April 5, 1993, article entitled "Illegal Child Labor Comes Back," *Fortune* magazine reported an increase in illegal child labor in America. Among other things, the magazine cites instances of children being "exploited," "exposed to danger," and otherwise being abused in sweatshops and on farms. As the article notes: "Child labor laws … are rarely enforced."

As federal and state laws now stand, if I were a nine-year-old child today, I could spend ten hours a day in the field chopping and picking cotton with no laws being broken, simply because I was working on a family farm.

Unfortunately, the advent of mechanized harvesting had not come about when I was a child, and bringing in a cotton crop required hard, grinding labor. I have heard grown men say it is the hardest work they have ever done. In Ammon Hennacy's essay "Picking Cotton," he states "I walked around searching for someone I might know, but my friends from the lettuce fields were wary of picking cotton, considering this the hardest job to be had and one to be taken only as a last resort."

As a small child working long hours in oppressive heat, exposed to pesticides and to extended hours of harmful sun rays as well as the pain of the repetitive motions required in chopping and picking cotton, I prayed for laws to be passed that would put an end to child labor. Being the daughter of a sharecropper who was forced, not by the government but by family circumstances, to toil long hours in the harsh cotton fields, I find it astonishing that the same federal and state laws still hold pertaining to family farms. The only significant exception is the compulsory school law, which is now enforced.

**Clara, age 14. Ready to go to the cotton patch.**

My least favorite month of the year was September. Not only were the cotton bolls open and ready for picking, but the school year started then as well. Since it was common during my parents' generation for children to help bring in the cotton crop, they thought nothing of keeping us out of school in September and October to work in the fields.

Living on the main county road, we saw the other kids pass by on the yellow school bus while we worked in the fields. I watched with envy as I looked up from my cotton row to see the bus pass by each day loaded with schoolchildren. I thought kids who got to go to school all year were the luckiest people on earth.

One of the advantages of farming on Crowley's Ridge was the hilly land, where the soil was much better suited to farming than the gumbo in the flat bottomland.

After we moved to New Castle, the farming arrangement between Daddy and our Uncle Elbert was little more than sharecropping. Since we didn't own farm equipment and Uncle Elbert owned a tractor, he used his tractor to help plant our cotton and corn. After the crops came up, he plowed them several times during the growing season. In exchange, Daddy agreed we would help him and his wife (my mother's sister) chop and pick their cotton.

There were also five children in their family, four girls and a boy—each one practically mirroring in age the five children in our family,. The big difference in the two families was this: They didn't expect their children to work in the fields as much as we did. They had only to help with chopping cotton in the summer months when school was out and didn't have to miss school in the fall to pick cotton. It was especially painful to stay out of school, picking their cotton while they were attending school, with us getting further behind each day in our own schoolwork.

I had a hard time watching our cousins get off the school bus in the afternoons, dressed in their nice school clothes while we were out in the fields picking their cotton. I didn't blame them or their parents for the circumstances, though; I only wished it could have been different.

❧

A particularly poignant memory occurred at the beginning of my senior year in high school. As the morning sun peeked over the horizon that September morning, I heard Mama's gentle voice as she entered the bedroom. "Toots, wake up. It's time to get up."

Unbeknownst to her, I was already awake and had tossed restlessly most of the night, fearful of what the morning might bring. As Mama and Daddy had talked at the breakfast table moments before, I had listened with dread as Daddy said, "It's time to get the kids up to go to the cotton field."

"What about Toots? Don't she need this full year of high school to get into college?" Mama asked. I had sucked in my breath, my heart pounding, as Daddy's fully anticipated, dreaded response came: "She's needed to help get the crop out."

There it was—that's all that had to be said—and my deepest fear was realized. We didn't question Daddy's decisions under *any* circumstances. In my family it was crystal clear to us kids that the adults made the decisions. And now my dream of becoming an elementary school teacher began to vanish as I struggled to hold back tears. Fortunately though, the intercessory prayers of my sister, Glenda, offered faithfully and lovingly, would play a role in events that would unfold later in unexpected ways.

It was September 1956, the first day of my senior year. I had hoped and prayed every day for months to be allowed to start school the first day of the school year and not be forced to miss weeks of school during the fall months as I had since the fourth grade.

Unable to afford to pay for outside labor and since our two eldest siblings were grown and had left home to be on their own, Daddy had no one to help harvest the cotton crop except my two younger sisters and me. But knowing that a commitment to any education beyond high school would place me away from home the next fall and the next crop anyway, I felt that Daddy could somehow manage without my help that current year too. But neither God nor prayers were to see it that way.

As a junior in the fall of the previous year, I had worked hard to overcome my late entrance to school and fortunately had managed to catch up with the class in schoolwork. Astonishingly, I was even awarded a four-year academic scholarship to Arkansas College at Batesville, but I would have to complete some required courses during my senior year in order to begin college coursework the next fall. Beginning those courses late by missing the first months of the school year would place me hopelessly behind.

Having spent my life up to that point laboring in hot cotton fields and then striving mightily each year to catch up quickly in school, I was no stranger to hard work and had learned early to cope with the handicap, common to that era, of being a farmer's daughter on a small farm. That, I thought, was my life and would be my future. What I didn't know was that my circumstances were destined to be instrumental in building within me a steely resolve to become successful in whatever the future held for me.

Child labor laws in effect throughout the United States in those years didn't apply to agricultural help of children living on parental farms. Arkansas' compulsory school attendance law was enacted in 1909 but was not widely enforced until 1959, two years after my high school graduation.

Many years later, my youngest sister, Glenda, revealed how she had prayed every day that I wouldn't have to miss the beginning months of my senior year. She had even begun to question God's existence when He didn't answer her repeated requests and thereafter went on to deny Him for many years. Glenda described her experience this way:

> Around the age of twelve I came to a crossroad in my life. During that summer of 1956, you, Mama, Marilyn, and I

attended the annual summer revival at our little Methodist church in New Castle. A little bit of conviction and a whole lot of terror—in that if I didn't *get saved* I would burn in hell forever—propelled me down the church aisle to shake the preacher's hand. I was *saved!* If I needed or wanted anything badly enough and if I prayed hard enough, it would happen. The preacher said that and I believed it.

You, Clara, were the smartest of all the girls. I was in awe of you because you *were* so smart and so determined to make a better life for yourself. You were also very kind and thoughtful toward me.

That fall, I knew Marilyn and I would have to stay out of school to pick cotton, and I accepted that, but even as young as I was, I understood how important it was for you not to have to miss certain classes your senior year. So I prayed, day after day, night after night, week after week: "Please God, don't let Clara have to stay out of school this year." When it didn't work out that way, I thought, *Thanks a lot God, I won't bother you anymore.*

Life went on. I got married and attended church regularly for years—taught Sunday school and vacation bible school, feeling basically the same way I felt that early fall morning when we got up and left for the field—betrayed by God.

Then one day about twenty or twenty-five years ago, I got it! God never told us He would do everything we wanted Him to do. He just promised to be with us and keep us strong during bad times.

Missing school to work in the fields was more the exception than the rule. Many students seemed to stigmatize classmates who missed school to help in the fields as somehow "different.". At that time, black and white students attended segregated schools. The black schools closed during the cotton picking season, but the white schools did not. Back then, how I wished our school closed during harvest as theirs did.

*Chapter 3*

♣

*School*

From the first heart-quickening mention of Daddy's observation that the crop had been mostly harvested and that "you kids need to get back in school," questions spilled from my lips. "What do you mean Daddy? Which day? Do you mean Monday of next week?"

To start school, we girls each got a couple of new dresses and a new pair of shoes. We always got the $5.99 dresses from West Brothers Department Store in Forrest City. The $5.99 dresses were ugly, but for $11.99 you could get a really pretty dress. We never got one of the more expensive dresses. The cheaper dresses were made from drab print fabric and had skimpy skirts and thin sashes. The $11.99 dresses, made from pretty pastel fabrics, had full, gathered skirts and wide sashes with white Peter Pan collars trimmed in delicate lace.

For my straight hair, my aunt sometimes gave me a Toni home permanent before I started school. The process took many hours since only a small strand of hair could be rolled onto each permanent wave roller. Aunt Goldie, a kind and patient person, took great pains to get each roller in position so the hair would stay wrapped around it until the setting lotion was applied. Finally, at the end of the day, I was proud to show off my soft curls—quite a change from my usual straight hair.

Though I loved to go to school and loved to learn, I always dreaded those first few weeks. I was already two months behind the other students, and even though I made good grades after catching up, it was an uphill struggle. Not only did my late start interrupt the learning process, it made it hard to adapt socially to the school environment. Unspoken worries—"Have the other kids formed into favorite groups of friends already? Who'll be my friend?"— were uppermost in my mind.

Each year I spent the first days of school looking around to see what the other students were doing in class. Following their lead, I took out pencil and paper, took notes, and attempted to do class assignments. At night I read the chapters they had already been through to get a better idea of what was needed to do the current class work and homework. I was usually up late at night after everyone else had gone to bed, and Mama or Daddy would sometimes call from their bedroom, "Toots, it's past your bedtime!" My response was to take a flashlight and books to my tiny bedroom and continue studying into the night.

Living in the country, I attended the local Parrott School through the fourth grade. Parrott was a two-room country school with the first and second grades in one room, and third and fourth grades in the other. The school's outdoor wooden toilets, one for girls and one for boys, were two-holers: two people could use them at the same time. Water came from an outdoor pump.

Though the accommodations were crude compared with today's schools, or even city schools back then, much of the knowledge I obtained at that little country school is still with me today. Attending Parrott School was a tremendous learning experience, both in terms of book knowledge and everyday living.

My fourth-grade teacher, Mrs. Cook, believed strongly in memory work. We were required to recite and spell states and capitals in alphabetical order in front of the entire class. My grandchildren are amazed that I can still name states and capitals today. Memorizing Bible verses to be quoted each Friday in Mrs. Cook's class was a standard assignment.

Mrs. Cook enjoyed her students and sometimes took two of the girls home to spend the weekend with her and her husband. When it was my time to go, I marveled at my first introduction to an indoor bathroom and my first bath in a gleaming white bathtub.

After finishing fourth grade at the Parrott country school, I was ready for the Forrest City school system and the fifth grade. Forrest City Elementary School was a large red-brick, two-story building in the middle of the city. This was a drastic change from the two-room school I had attended in first through fourth grades. I was amazed to find that each class was held in a separate room. There was even a stage in the large auditorium.

Riding a school bus twenty miles round trip over gravel roads made for a long day. Waiting for the bus that first morning of the school year always made my stomach turn over. My nerves would be on edge as questions came to mind: "How far behind will I be? Will I be able to catch up with the rest of the class? Will I be able to find my classrooms and the bathroom? How will the other students react to me?"

The end of the school day each afternoon also proved to be an anxious time. What would happen if I was delayed gathering up my books to take home? What if the bus driver left a few minutes early, and I missed the bus? There was no phone at home to call anybody.

As a fifth grader entering the city school system, I walked into a classroom full of students. It was my first day of school but not the first day of the school year. When I entered the classroom, Mrs. Moseley, my homeroom teacher, told me to have a seat. I stood motionless, in shock, in front of the largest classroom I had ever seen. In reality, it was probably a small classroom with no more than twenty children, but to someone from a two-room school, it was a frightening experience.

Mrs. Moseley had to tell me for a second time to sit down. As I took a seat in the back of the room, all eyes seemed to stare at my every move. I thought I heard a snicker from a group of girls as I passed their desk, but I kept my head down and dared not look at them.

I found here my first experience with perceived discrimination—but not because of skin color. Only the poorer kids missed school to *pick cotton.* Some of the students wouldn't dare be seen talking to me or even acknowledging my presence.

In my mind the school catered to the "city kids" and seemed to consider it a waste of time to give children of sharecroppers individual attention. In retrospect, I can see that I wasn't really a good judge of what others thought; it was what *I thought* they were thinking that made me miserable.

The whole situation fostered intense preoccupation with feelings of fear and with wondering what others thought about my entering school late. Looking back, I can see that I let my imagination get away from me. It was an inward battle, fought silently, as my parents came from a generation where it was usual for children to join in the harvest. That generation knew little of the differing socioeconomic classes within the schools and the perceived need to be from one of the admired groups.

We were always careful not to reveal one word of how we felt to our parents. We knew they also did without things that they needed at times, and there was really no one else to help out but us. As they struggled to make a living and to keep food on the table, we didn't want to heap additional pain on them.

As children, we were pulled mentally in two opposite directions. At home we felt we were doing something important by helping put food on the table, thereby instilling a sense of value to what we did. But at school, the kids seemed to value having soft hands and milk-white skin with no tan or freckles and wearing pretty rings and pretty clothes from the best stores. No wonder we felt we were from a different world.

The more aware I became of the difference between the city kids and the country kids, the more self-conscious I became. The city kids seemed more like one big family, visiting each other's homes, attending the same churches, and going to other classmates' houses for birthday parties.

It never occurred to me that their lifestyle was dictated by convenience just as mine was dictated by the inconvenience of living miles away from the city. I thought they were better than me because they lived in "nicer" homes and had "better" clothes. It took many years to overcome these feelings and break down the barriers I had erected.

∞

The elementary school in Forrest City went through the sixth grade. Graduating from elementary to junior high school was a big event. While practicing for the program, I heard some of the girls describing the new dresses they planned to wear for graduation. Of course, this presented a problem for me because I had nothing new—or even nice—to wear. Mama had ordered some dress material from the Sears catalog, but even if it arrived promptly, there would hardly be enough time to make a dress.

When the last week of the school year arrived, we attended school on Monday and Tuesday and were scheduled to go back a half day that Friday for graduation. Since our cotton crop was ready to chop, we spent Wednesday and Thursday working in the field. Sadly, my thoughts were centered on walking across the stage at graduation on Friday wearing my old clothes.

When we went home for lunch on Thursday, I walked

into my bedroom and saw the most beautiful dress hanging on the door. I knew immediately the material had arrived in the mail from Sears, and unknown to me, Mama had spent many hours making the dress for my graduation.

The dress was made of a pale lilac organdy material. It had tucks sewn in the full, gathered skirt with a wide sash that tied in the back. I could hardly wait to wear it to school the next day. The dress was my very favorite, not only because it was pretty, but also because I knew Mama had made a special effort to have it ready for my graduation. .

ख/১

**Forrest City High School**

When I entered junior high and the courses became more difficult, some of the teachers tried to discourage me from taking the harder courses since I started late in the school year.

As I attempted to enroll in algebra class, I timidly

approached the teacher, Mr. Lieblong. "I suggest you think about taking an easier math course because algebra will be too hard after missing so many classes. You won't be able to catch up with the other students," he said. "Can I just try it?" I asked. At the end of the school year, Mr. Lieblong asked me to stop by his desk after class. "Congratulations on making As and Bs in my class this year," he said.

During my senior year when I found I again wouldn't be starting school at the beginning of the year, I bought the same typing book the students used in school; then I found an old manual typewriter for two dollars and taught myself to type.

As I entered typing class that November day and nervously approached Mrs. Henderson, the typing teacher, she said, "I can't allow you to take typing because you are already too far behind and you may hold up the other students." Not about to give up easily, I begged, "Will you give me a chance? I think I can do it." She said, "Yes, you can try, but you need to be thinking of another course you can take rather than typing."

To Mrs. Henderson's surprise, I was at least as far along as the other students in the class. Not only did I finish the year with all As, but she chose me and my best friend, Bonita, as assistants to help with grading papers and other tasks, giving us extra credit for honors.

By the beginning of the second semester each year, because of my hard work and my ability to catch up and make good grades, many of the teachers seemed to forget my first semester and averaged my year-end grades based on the second semester only.

Being a conscientious student, I impressed some of the teachers with my passion for learning and sometimes became teacher's pet. This was quite a contrast to my home environment, where I was accustomed to receiving little attention and even less emphasis on education. I would be encouraged with my accomplishments at the end of each school year, but sadly, history would repeat itself the next fall.

One of the worst days of my life came during the spring of my senior year when annual selections for the National Honor Society were announced during an assembly before the entire school. My best friend Bonita's name was announced, and then my cousin Jo Ann, who lived across the road from me, was selected. Since we were all good students and made similar grades, I felt my name would be called at any minute. When that didn't happen, I was devastated. My grades were good, and I had worked extremely hard to overcome missing the first two months of school.

"What's wrong?" Mama asked when I got off the school bus with red, puffy eyes that afternoon. I didn't get selected for the National Honor Society," I managed to say. "We all know you deserve to be in the Honor Society," Mama said with tears in her eyes also. My stomach churning, I couldn't eat anything that night, unable to cope with the hurt. When I awakened the next morning, my pillow was still wet from tears shed during the night.

I later got the courage to ask Miss Davidson, one of my favorite teachers, if she knew why I wasn't selected for the Honor Society. "School attendance is one of the factors taken into consideration in making the selections," she told me kindly. "I was so sorry you were not selected because you are a good student. I wish it could have been different," she said. Making the Honor Society would have meant the world to me.

ॐ

Small in population, with about twelve thousand people, Forrest City had always been a cliquish place, as was the school. While growing up and attending school, I never felt I really belonged there. Nor did I ever feel I belonged laboring in the fields. Working in the fields alongside my parents and siblings, however, later helped inspire my long, successful career. Picking and chopping cotton were great motivators.

While working in the fields, I daydreamed for hours about getting off the farm. I couldn't wait to escape. All those years of working up and down the cotton rows, I was planning my future, and that future had nothing to do with farms or cotton or backaches. More than once during my professional career in later years, I was told that I had unusual spark and determination.

Envisioning myself as a schoolteacher, I dreamed of recognizing and helping underprivileged children. At a young age, perhaps influenced by my own experiences, I had a vision that centered on providing educational opportunities for children who had been ditched by society. I wanted to help them discover their uniqueness and talents, to encourage them to believe in themselves, and to teach them to strive to reach their full potential regardless of their backgrounds.

*Chapter 4*

♣

*Rural Deliveries*

On a hot summer day in the country, we eagerly waited for the big flatbed ice truck to come lumbering down the gravel road and pull up in our driveway. When he finally arrived the iceman used huge tongs to pick up a fifty-pound block of ice from the back of the truck and sling it into our icebox.

Usually made of wood for ease of construction and insulation, household iceboxes had hollow walls lined with tin or zinc and packed with insulating materials like cork, sawdust, or straw. The large block of ice sat in a tray or compartment near the top of the icebox. Cold air circulated down and around storage compartments in the lower section. In cheaper models like ours, a drip pan placed under the box had to be emptied daily. An ice pick chipped the desired amount of ice from the large block. We used the ice sparingly, as it would be another week before the iceman made his rounds again.

It was an exciting day when we finally got a used refrigerator. We quickly learned to refill the metal ice-cube trays after each meal, since neglecting to do so would result in no ice for the next meal.

Perhaps the most anticipated event on the farm was the weekly appearance of the rolling store. Made of a large improvised truck or old school bus, the rectangular store was long and narrow inside with shelves on each side.

The rolling store was common in rural areas populated with sharecroppers and families on small farms. Traveling on the dusty gravel roads, winding through the countryside, rolling stores had regular routes so customers knew when to expect the truck.

Each clutching a penny or maybe a nickel, hoping to have enough money to buy some candy, we waited as the rolling store approached. While we spent considerable time making the difficult decision of whether to buy a piece of candy or a piece of bubble gum, Mama stepped inside to make her purchases. She bought such staples as sugar, flour, baking powder, salt, canned goods, and sewing thread. The store also sold hardware: nails, screws, tools, and the like.

Flour was sold in fifty-pound bags and lard in twenty-five-pound buckets. After the flour was used, the colorful cotton flour sacks made nice aprons for Mama and underwear for us girls. In a large farming family, nothing was wasted.

In the winter, we met the rolling store with an empty jug to buy kerosene. The jug was filled from a big kerosene tank on the back of the rolling store, and we used the kerosene to heat our cook stove and to burn in the oil lamps.

While we periodically made the ten-mile trip into town for supplies, the rolling store was an added convenience—and a necessity at times when we couldn't get to town to shop. If there was no money available, we sometimes swapped eggs or fresh vegetables for staples from the rolling store.

In the spring when the rural mail carrier honked his horn for someone to come to the mailbox, it usually meant Mama's order of live baby chickens had arrived. Delivered in a cardboard box with ventilation holes poked in the top, the poor chicks would barely be alive. We tried to nurse them back to health by giving them water from a medicine dropper but usually lost some of the weaker chicks.

Surviving chicks would provide eggs and, later on, Sunday dinner in the form of fried chicken. Although the mature chickens didn't look like the cute baby chicks, I couldn't watch as Mama or Daddy laid a chicken's head on a block and chopped it off with an axe or wrung its head off by twisting the chicken around and around. However, the grown chicks provided our favorite meal of fried chicken, mashed potatoes, and a big plate of sliced tomatoes fresh from the garden.

Twice each year we anxiously checked the mailbox for arrival of the latest Sears Roebuck catalog. Receiving the catalog—especially the Christmas catalog—was one of the highlights of the summer and winter seasons. After a few weeks, the pages of the catalogs would be curled due to overuse. As soon as a new catalog arrived, the old one was promptly taken to the outhouse for another use. Anyone who has ever lived in the country and used an outhouse knows what it means to run out of the black-and-white pages of the catalog and have only the colored pages left!

I spent hours lying on my bed staring into that wish book. I studied girls' clothes in the catalog, imagining what it would be like to have a different dress to wear each day of the school week. I secretly made out catalog order forms listing my favorite outfits along with prices and sizes, hoping the list wouldn't be found.

Mama occasionally ordered clothes for us when money was available. At Christmas we each selected one small toy from the catalog. I remember cutting out the picture of a Betsy Wetsy doll. I was delighted to find my very own doll under the tree on Christmas morning.

*Chapter 5*

❧

*Daily Life on the Farm*

We chopped and cultivated our cotton in June and July. In August, we helped Mama can vegetables from the garden and fruit from local orchards. Gardening was hard work, but at the same time, it provided our main food supply from spring into the fall months. We picked and shelled bushel baskets full of peas, butter beans, and green beans for canning. After shelling peas and beans all day, our fingers would be stained, sore, and swollen.

A trip to the cornfield in early summer provided one of my favorite fresh vegetables. I didn't know for years that what we called "roastnears" were the "roasting-ears size" of corn pulled from the leafy cornstalks. A meal of fresh corn on the cob or fried corn cut from the cob was delicious.

We liked the taste of all the fresh vegetables, especially tomatoes. We ate tomatoes off and on all day when they were in season. We could go to the garden, pull a big red ripe tomato off the vine, and eat it on the spot. Long after most people had abandoned their gardens in the fall, we found late green tomatoes still clinging to long tomato vines. Pulling them from the vines, we wrapped them individually in old newspaper and stored them in a cardboard box under the bed, where they eventually ripened. Not as tasty as vine-ripened tomatoes, they still provided fresh vegetables long into the winter.

We picked cucumbers from the vines and watched as Mama soaked them overnight in a brine of salt water. The next day she stuffed the cucumbers in jars and covered them with a prepared solution of vinegar and pickling spices. The transformation of cucumbers into pickles provided a condiment we wouldn't normally have.

Peach orchards surrounded Forrest City, especially the New Castle area. As a child, I never fully appreciated the scope of the peach processing operation and the financial impact it had on the area.

Living about a mile from the peach shed at the large Summer Sweet Orchard, we smelled the perfume of squashed peaches fermenting in the summer heat filling the air. Peaches were everywhere. Going to the orchard and picking our own peaches for canning was a hot and itchy job. Regardless of how careful we were, peach fuzz covered our skin and got inside our clothing.

Peeling and canning peaches was a summer tradition. We spent many hours on the front porch of the New Castle house peeling peaches in a large washtub. We filled the tub half full of water drawn from the cistern and emptied the peaches into the water. After a while the tub would be so full of peach peelings and peach seeds that it had to be emptied and refilled with fresh water.

My sisters and I peeled the peaches while Mama cooked and canned them. Some of the peaches looked too good to pass up, so we ate them on the spot as we peeled them. Because of my skinny hands and arms, I was also assigned the job of washing and scrubbing most of the canning jars since only my hands fit easily inside the jars.

❧

Since Daddy loved to hunt and fish, we had fresh fish to eat in the summer and wild game, such as squirrel and rabbit, to eat during winter. A platter of fried squirrel or a pot of squirrel and dumplings was a welcome treat.

Catfish, crappie, and other types of fish caught from local lakes and sloughs was a welcome addition to our diet. We loved Mama's fried fish but had to watch for small bones, especially in the crappie. It wasn't unusual for us to get tiny fish bones lodged in our throats. Mama would have us eat something coarse like cornbread to dislodge it.

∽

Hog killing day on the farm was a big event. We waited until the weather turned cold so the meat wouldn't spoil. Only the more affluent among us had freezers, so in order to preserve the meat, Daddy salted it and then hung it from the barn rafters so rodents couldn't get to it. A neighbor or two helped with killing and dressing the heavy hogs, lifting them into a barrel of scalding water to remove the hair. Payment to the neighbors came in the form of some of the fresh meat for them to take home.

I always looked forward to the fresh meat but hated hearing the hogs squeal as they were being killed. Daddy's sharp butcher knives were used to cut the hogs' throats. Crawling under the bed and covering my ears to keep from hearing the desperate high-pitched squeals didn't help at all. Later, after the meat was dressed, it didn't look like Betsy anymore (or whatever name we had given to the hog), but it tasted so good.

Very little of a butchered hog went to waste. The lungs and liver, sometimes called "liver and lights," were cooked to provide some of the first fresh meat from hog killing day. Since these body parts of Betsy's didn't look or sound appetizing, I declined to eat them. Hog brains, which were prepared with scrambled eggs, also fell into that category as far as my appetite was concerned.

My favorite part of the fresh meat was pork tenderloin that Mama fried, usually the day after butchering. Tenderloin is the choice part of the hog. As its name indicates, it is tender and tasty. Country ham also fits into that category. As different from ordinary ham as night is from day, country ham is the aristocrat of pig meat. The whole ham is cured for several months while it sheds moisture and its favor increases. Sandwiched inside a fluffy buttermilk biscuit, country ham, along with a bowl of red-eye gravy, is a Southern classic.

We set aside certain parts of the hog for making sausage. Cut into small pieces, the pork was fed into the sausage grinder. We all took turns at the sausage grinder, eagerly anticipating the delicious country sausage that would be the result. Once a large dishpan of meat was finely ground, Mama and Daddy mixed it with pepper and sage and shaped it into patties.

The taste of real homemade sausage is vastly different from sausage bought in stores. The fresh meat and seasonings give it a richer taste found only in homemade sausage. Mama sometimes canned some of the sausage patties to use later.

Hog intestines, commonly called chitterlings, and a meal of some of the better cuts of meat, were given to our friend Judy, a nice black lady who lived across the road from us. Since Judy had fig and apple trees and always shared her fruit with us, we made sure she got some of the fresh meat.

We cut skin and any fat attached to the skin of the hog into small pieces. Using a large black iron pot in the backyard, Daddy rendered the pork skins and fat, which usually provided enough cooking lard to last through the winter. The remaining crisp pork skins, called cracklins, were used to make cracklin cornbread. In later years, cracklins became a popular commercial snack known as pork rinds.

❧

In addition to working in the fields, we had other chores to do each day. During school months, we got home around four thirty, changed clothes, and started our chores. In the wintertime Daddy cut and split wood to form a large woodpile. One of our daily chores was to bring wood from the pile and stack it on the front porch for burning in the wood stove.

The wood stove was our source of heat and worked fine if we stood close to the stove, but it was necessary to turn around to get our backsides warm. If we stood too long without turning around, our skin would become blotchy purple from the heat. Marilyn, Glenda, and I had a regular bedtime routine during cold winter months. Dressed in flannel pajamas, we heated our pillows by the stove and then jumped into bed and snuggled together like three spoons.

Another daily chore was feeding corn to the chickens. Going to the corncrib in the barn, we got ears of dried corn to shell for the chickens to eat. One day as Marilyn and Glenda walked into the corncrib, a large diamondback rattlesnake lay coiled, its rattlers buzzing, ready to strike. They both froze, but Glenda managed to get out, *"Snake!"* They dropped the corn and ran from the barn screaming, knowing how fortunate they were not to have been bitten.

We lived in fear of stepping on a rattlesnake in the fields or feeling fangs sink into our hands as we reached for a boll of cotton or a vegetable in the garden. Our closet neighbor, Mabel, was bitten by a rattlesnake once as she was picking beans in her garden. Mabel survived the bite but was hospitalized in poor condition for several days.

Walking through tall grass we sometimes encountered blue racer snakes and ran away screaming. These snakes seemed to run toward us, so that was what we told each other; and we really believed that blue racers chased us. Long green snakes called garden snakes were common. We were told they were harmless, but we gave them plenty of room.

Gathering eggs from the henhouse was also one of our daily chores. Trying to get eggs out from under a hen without getting pecked was one of the more challenging tasks. Inside the chicken house, we also had to watch for long black chicken snakes wrapped around the poles the chickens used for roosting.

Another challenge was getting chased by roosters with long spurs. We figured if we fell and he caught up with us, we would be as good as dead—or at least blind from him pecking our eyes out. If one of the roosters took out after us, we wasted no time running into the house by way of the back porch, leaping over the steps, and grabbing for the safety of the screen door. The same thing was true for the bull in the pasture; we wondered if we could make it over the fence before he reached us and gored us to our death.

And who could forget the electric fence? Neighborhood kids lined up holding onto it, and the one on the very end got the worst shock. Just barely touching the wire shocked us badly, but if we grabbed it hard and held tight, only a dull shock went through us. Now I can see how dangerous that must have been to our hearts—but we didn't know it then.

Picking blackberries and dewberries to take home for Mama to make a berry cobbler was part of summertime life on the farm. Keeping in mind that the berry patches were a natural habitat for snakes made us extremely careful about where we stepped. The berry vines covered with briers scratched our arms and hands until they sometimes bled, but Mama's delicious cobblers were well worth the pain.

Plum thickets were also some of our favorite places. The plum trees or bushes were not much taller than we were so we shook them to make the plums fall to the ground. Picking them up, we filled shoeboxes with the delicious red and yellow fruit, eating our fill of the wild plums on the way home. If enough of the plums were left, Mama used them to make plum jelly.

Muscadine jelly made from wild muscadines, also called scuppernongs, was another favorite. Daddy filled the pockets of his hunting coat with muscadines found in the woods while rabbit hunting or squirrel hunting and brought them home for making jelly. None of the muscadines went to waste, as hulls made muscadine preserves and the soft fruit inside made delicious jelly.

The wonderful smells of navy beans and cornbread cooking in Mama's kitchen, of a barn filled with fresh hay, and of a dusty road with a light sprinkle of rain are favorite scents reminiscent of country life.

We always had a large potato patch alongside the garden. We dreaded digging potatoes among the fat potato bugs each year. Daddy plowed the potatoes in rows, and we dug them out of the plowed dirt with our bare hands. When he plowed the potatoes, his manic depression kicked in, and he cursed and yelled, although we were doing the best we could.

One time while digging potatoes, I was on the receiving end of his razor tongue. He didn't know I had a huge boil, the size of a silver dollar, at the base of my right buttock. When I got on my knees to dig the potatoes out of the dirt, the heel of my shoe would strike the boil, causing extreme pain.

By the time we got home for lunch that day the boil had ruptured. When Mama asked what was wrong, I poured out the morning's events, including Daddy's actions. Evidently, Mama told him what I said. Later, when we sat down to lunch, Daddy shook his finger at me and said, "Don't you ever complain to your mother about what I do again." To this day I still have a one-inch scar from the boil.

Some years we planted a patch of peanuts. When the stalks were pulled up, the green peanuts clinging to the plants needed to dry before they were edible. Many a stomachache occurred from our sneaking handfuls of the green peanuts before they were dry enough to eat safely.

Colds and the flu were a part of life in the winter. When we were unlucky enough to get colds, sore throats, or the flu, these illnesses sometimes resulted in cases of the croup. Mama rubbed Vicks salve on our chests at night and made croup rags from the Vicks salve, which she pinned to the underside of our night clothes. There were no doctor visits.

ᴄᴦ

Grapevines in the woods were our modern-day swing sets. Swinging on a grapevine in the woods was fun, but finding one that went out over some water (or something else dangerous) was the most fun of all. Getting the vine going really high and then letting go to see who could jump the farthest was our version of the Olympics.

We also used the grapevines for our crude attempts at smoking. Small grapevines with hollow centers were lit and smoked. The holes in the vines were sometimes too big, and if you drew hard on the vine, you'd come close to also pulling a small flame into your mouth and end up with a badly scorched tongue. The positive side of this experiment: I have never since had a desire to smoke.

It was a miracle that none of the five of us kids was ever seriously injured; we had no broken bones, and we rarely developed serious illnesses. However we all came down with the usual childhood diseases: German measles, red measles, mumps, pinkeye, and chicken pox. Ill for several weeks, I suffered most from chicken pox and, according to Mama, was "out of my head" part of the time.

ᴄᴦ

One of the perils of living in the country was my allergic reaction to poison ivy. The consequence of a day playing in the woods during the summer was usually an extreme outbreak. In fact I could recognize poison oak and poison ivy plants and would avoid them as if they were poisonous snakes. Many times I even came down with bad cases of poison ivy when I had not been in the woods and never knew how I contacted the plant.

Once, poison ivy blisters the size of each palm covered both of my hands, and long blisters between my fingers prevented me from bending them. Daddy took his knife and opened the blisters to drain the fluid, which, as horrifying as it sounds, was actually a relief because they had been so tight and full of fluid that they were very painful.

Another serious outbreak of poison ivy occurred when I was six years old. I was covered from head to toe with poison ivy, even inside my mouth. For two weeks, I neither ate nor slept. I tried to drink small amounts of fluid through a straw but couldn't close my mouth far enough to use the straw effectively. When red streaks ran up my arms underneath the skin, Mama and Daddy took me to the doctor. Though the doctor said it was the worst case of poison ivy he had ever treated, he didn't admit me to the hospital.

Mama and Daddy took me back to the doctor each day for an injection. After two weeks of misery, the poison ivy finally cleared up. It was only years later that my brother admitted that, as a boyish prank, he had rubbed a poison ivy plant over my body, creating the severe outbreak. At only six, I had not yet learned to recognize the plant.

⌇

We usually had at least one cow that provided dairy products for the family: milk, butter, and buttermilk. The taste of fresh milk straight from the cow was very different from pasteurized milk. Sometimes the cow would eat wild onions or bitter weeds, causing the milk to taste like the onions or bitter weeds.

We also churned our own butter using the cow's milk. We hated churning. It sometimes led to arguments over everyone not doing their share. The churn was a two-foot-tall pottery crock with a top that had a hole in the middle for the dasher to go through. The dasher moved up and down, turning the clabbered milk in the churn into butter. When the churned butter started floating in clumps on top of the milk, it was declared ready, and Mama would dip it out and put it in a butter mold to create designs—stars, shells, moons, and more.

ↄ

We liked going to the watermelon patch on hot summer days and thumping on watermelons to see if they were ripe. Once the thumping sounded just right, we dropped the watermelon to the ground to break it open and get the "heart" out. The heart was the sweetest and tastiest part of the melon. Then, sitting on the ground eating, we would see who could spit melon seeds the farthest. The watermelon rinds were given to the hogs.

During summer months, when we were not working in the field, we swam in nearby Village Creek. Uncomfortable with us going near water without adult supervision, which was not always available, Mama seldom allowed us to go swimming in the creek. Tongue in cheek, Mama would say, "You kids don't need to get around water until you learn how to swim."

We played hopscotch, jump rope, playhouse, and other outside games. Our playhouses consisted of clean-swept areas among the trees. The furniture was foot-long boards resting on empty tin cans, which were sometimes stacked to make improvised cabinets or other pieces of furniture or appliances. On rainy days, we played games of jacks on the linoleum living room floor to keep busy.

One word you never, *ever* heard from us was "bored." We were happy and content to be around the house and not in the cotton patch. As long as we were under a shade tree, we thought it was cool regardless of how high the temperature rose. The same can be said for being inside the house without air conditioning or even an electric fan.

☙

I remember sleeping with the windows open in summer, hearing crickets chirping and frogs croaking. If a car went down the road late after we were in bed, we smelled the faint scent of dust coming in the raised window. If rain started during the night, the mist entering the window and settling on us had a clean smell to it.

The peaceful sound of steady, light raindrops on a tin roof and the frightening sound of hard raindrops or hail on the same roof would either lull us to sleep or keep us wide-awake. During cotton chopping season, we thought rain on the tin roof was the most beautiful sound on earth because it usually meant it would be too wet to chop cotton the next day.

☙

Occasionally, a horse or cow would die in the neighbor's pasture behind our house. It would be pulled by a rope behind the tractor to a place far from the house and left to decay. Neighborhood kids took turns daring each other to see who could get closest to it without gagging or vomiting. Giant buzzards settled down to scavenge the meat, and it was hard not to turn away as they pecked at the decaying flesh. The same kids would return later to look at the ribs sticking up and the mass of giant leg bones.

∽

Walking under a wooden country bridge as a vehicle approached and letting it drive over the bridge with us under it was a "double-dog-dare" event. Terrified while listening to the thumping of the planks, which never seemed to be nailed down as the tires rolled over them, I would promise myself if I got out alive, I would never do it again. However, like the thrilling but scary ride of a rollercoaster, we were all ready to do it again as soon as another car came by.

Fond memories often come to mind of late summer evenings we four sisters spent lying on a blanket in the front yard trying to make out shapes in the clouds, such as "that one looks like a………" As night approached, each of us tried to be the first to spot a star in the darkening sky. The first to see a star inevitably recited, "Star light, star bright, first star I've seen tonight, wish I may, wish I might have the wish I wish tonight." She would then make a wish, feeling there was an outside chance of the wish coming true.

Once darkness fell, we caught lightning bugs in Mason jars until mosquitoes ran us inside the house. Then Mama got the DDT-filled hand sprayer and sprayed each room to kill the mosquitoes that had managed to get in the house. Naturally, we—as well as most scientists at that early date— were oblivious to the harmful effects of DDT on humans.

∽

Before the advent of the Salk vaccine, contracting polio, a highly contagious illness, was a constant fear of childhood. Since the cause of polio was not widely known, Mama and Daddy used the threat of polio (real or imagined) as a reason to keep us from engaging in various activities.

Mama warned us about wading in muddy country ponds because we might get polio; however, we still splashed around the shores of nearby ponds with horses and cows standing on the other side at the water's edge. We told ourselves they would never come over to the side where we were, just as we told ourselves the snakes in the pond would drown if they opened their mouths to bite us.

Listening to the radio one day in 1952, I heard my favorite newscaster, Edward R. Murrow, state, "Tomorrow's headlines will be the Salk polio vaccine." Gathering around the radio the next day, we heard the announcement that Dr. Jonas Salk had discovered a successful polio vaccine.

The vaccine was made public in 1955 and couldn't have come at a better time. In 1952 alone, the Centers for Disease Control estimated there were over twenty-one thousand cases of polio in the United States. The public had become increasingly frightened of this disease, also called infantile paralysis, which was crippling and even killing people. With gratitude from the entire world, Dr. Salk's vaccine put a stop to the polio epidemic.

∽

Washday was a busy day around our house. If we were not working in the fields, we helped Mama with the weekly chore. In the earlier days, Mama washed clothes on a rubboard or washboard. The washboard was a rectangular wooden frame holding a section of galvanized metal formed into rows of upraised horizontal ridges. Clothes were hand scrubbed against the ridged surface of the board.

Mama built a fire and got a large iron pot of water going in the backyard to boil the more heavily soiled clothes. She put what she called "bluing" in it. I never knew the purpose of the bluing and thought maybe it was just something people had done since pioneer days that had never died out or, as some thought, that it was to lessen fading and to make whites whiter.

We later acquired a wringer washer. A big improvement over the rubboard, the wringer washer eliminated manually scrubbing and wringing the clothes. Mama filled the washer with water, added washing powder, and let the clothes agitate for a few minutes. She used Duz washing powder, not only because it was the least expensive, but also because the large box often contained a dish or dish towel. The clothes were then fed through the wringer, two hard rubber rollers, and into a tub of rinse water.

Clothes seemed to often get hung up in the wringer, and it would have to be disassembled to get them out. We were warned not to touch the wringer rollers while they were turning due to the danger of getting our fingers caught. Occasionally, we would hear a rumor of that happening, leaving the impression that someone had lost a finger—or maybe even a hand!

After washing the clothes, we hung them on the outdoor clothesline to dry. Washday was usually a Monday since we never hung clothes outside on the weekend, especially not on Sunday. Sunday was considered a religious day of rest.

We hung the clothes in a certain order—whites first (I don't know why)—and only whites with whites. Sheets and towels were hung on the outside lines so we could hide our unmentionables in the middle. The most efficient way to hang clothes was to line them up so that each item didn't need two clothespins but shared one clothespin with the next washed item on the line. When we ran out of room on the clothesline, we threw the wet clothes over a barbed wire fence, a bush, or whatever was handy. Mama used the leftover rinse water to mop the kitchen floor.

We gathered the dry clothes off the line before "dusky dark," so the clothes wouldn't become damp in the night air. If the temperature was below freezing, the clothes would "freeze dry" but then had to be brought inside and hung over chair backs around the wood heater to dry as they began to thaw.

Since most clothes were 100 percent cotton and starched when washed, they had to be sprinkled and ironed, which in the early years we did with flat irons or smoothing irons heated on the stove. Mama did most of the ironing since the flat irons were heavy, cumbersome, and very hot.

Later, after we got a fancy, lightweight electric iron, we were more willing to help with the ironing since it was much easier than with the heavy flat irons. Memories of Mama standing at the old ironing board ironing clothes and listening to *Stella Dallas* or some other radio soap opera are still with me today.

*Chapter 6*

♣

*Teenage Years*

We continued to farm as Bill finished high school and afterward joined the Navy. That left the four girls to help with the cotton crop—but only for a short time.

Mama was excited when Maxine started dating at age fifteen. I always felt Mama relived her courting days vicariously through her daughters. Daddy vehemently opposed Maxine's dating at such a young age. When she had a date, Daddy left the house so he wouldn't have to meet her suitor. After Maxine and her date left, Daddy always came back and went on a tirade. He and Mama yelled at each other for what seemed like hours. Mama always fought for Maxine and her boyfriends.

Daddy never liked any of the boys Maxine went out with, and I always dreaded hearing she had a date. On one occasion, I knew she had a date with her current boyfriend, Bob. I also knew Daddy disapproved of him. When Bob drove up the driveway and Maxine wasn't quite ready to go, I went outside before he had a chance to get out of the car and told him she wasn't home. I don't think Bob believed me, but he left. My sister yelled at me later, but that was better than listening to my parents fight.

When I was in tenth grade, Maxine married. At seventeen she met and married her husband, Gene, in Memphis. Daddy finally met Gene before they married. Sitting on the living room couch, Daddy told Gene, "I don't want her to marry and move away because I need her to help with the cotton crop." Years later, Daddy and Gene became close, as they enjoyed hunting and fishing together.

My interest in the opposite sex was slow to develop, partly because of a lack of self-confidence and partly because of the experience with Daddy and Maxine. I decided it wasn't worth the hassle.

However, during my senior year, Jimmy, the brother

of our longtime local sheriff, asked me out on a date. On that first date, Jimmy and I saw a movie entitled *Shotgun Wedding* where the father of the bride came to the front door of a farmhouse with his shotgun and threatened to shoot the groom-to-be. Jokingly, I leaned over to Jimmy and said, "My Daddy is just like that man in the movie. He has a shotgun like that one."

When Jimmy took me home that night, he walked me to the front porch, said goodnight very quickly, and ran back to his car. I didn't have to worry about him sticking around too long and getting "fresh." We dated occasionally but lost touch after high school.

During school months, we could ride the school bus to the city library during lunchtime once a week. I always went and stayed as long as I could, checking out as many books as possible. I can still remember the faint musty smell of the library and the excitement of being around all those books. Books were my salvation and the library, my refuge. I devoured every book I could get my hands on. My idea of having a big time was reading a good book.

We also had a library at the school, but I had read almost every book there—classics like *Little Women*, *Gone with the Wind*, and all of Laura Ingalls Wilder's books. During high school, I considered it an honor when I was selected to work in the school library for extra credit.

ॐ

Growing up, we attended Forrest Chapel Methodist Church, a small community church in New Castle. Attending church provided the main social connection in our otherwise isolated lives. I looked forward to the fellowship among church members and the preacher's assurance that God was watching over us. After entering high school, I volunteered as church secretary for several years, helping on Sundays with totaling and posting attendance and collections figures.

Sunday services were an unquestioned routine for Mama and us kids. She always made sure the whole family went to church every Sunday with the exception of Daddy. He refused to go to church, but since Mama didn't drive, he took us each Sunday and picked us up afterward.

Growing up, as I said my nightly prayers, I prayed that Daddy would start going to church. He never did. Having listened to our preacher's sermons describing how you would burn in hell if you were not saved, I was afraid Daddy would die and go to hell. I loved Daddy and was concerned about what might happen to him. I have yet to come to a clear decision concerning what I was taught in church in those early years, but the comfort and inspiration that little church provided when I was growing up is still with me today.

The local custom of having the preacher come to your home for Sunday dinner rotated among the church members. Because Daddy wouldn't attend church and didn't want anything to do with the preacher, Mama was reluctant to take her turn. I begged her not to volunteer, realizing how embarrassing it would be for Daddy to pick us up from church and then disappear, refusing to have lunch with us; however, she felt guilty about not doing her part.

The one time we did have the preacher for Sunday dinner, Daddy was nowhere to be found. After taking us home from church, he left the house before the preacher got there. Later, I was terribly embarrassed when one of the neighbors laughingly told me that the preacher knew exactly why my dad was not there.

೧

For some reason, many of the small children in the church were drawn to me and begged their parents for permission to sit with me during services. Their parents allowed them to sit with me as long as they behaved. Sometimes there were two or three children sitting on either side of me during services. Some of the more prominent families in the community often asked me to babysit. I loved children, and many of them in the area seemed to love me as well.

During my junior year of high school I was contacted by Russell Horton, a former member of the church, who, along with his wife Martha, had moved to Bethesda, Maryland. Russell, for whom I had babysat, was the administrator of a large hospital in Bethesda.

Russell wrote a long letter inquiring of my interest in accepting a grant from the hospital to attend college there and major in early childhood services. He said all my expenses would be taken care of by the hospital. He wrote that he thought I had a special gift for dealing with children and wanted to know if I would consider pursuing this field. I would, of course, be obligated to work at his hospital for a limited number of years after graduation. I was flattered, but to my mind going to Maryland to go to school and work would have been comparable to me going to a foreign country today. I graciously declined the offer.

*Chapter 7*

♣

*Inclement Weather*

Spring and fall winds, rain, hail, and sleet rattled boards, pushed up the roof, and whistled around the corners of our old farmhouse, sitting square atop the hills of Eastern Arkansas' Crowley's Ridge. The sound of weather was often scary, and scary weather was a big part of life on the farm.

We listened to the weatherman on the radio morning, noon, and night as he announced fair skies or inclement weather. The meaning of those two words, big ones for us kids, was as familiar as pop stars' names are to girls today, for the weather affected the farm's days and nights and especially the crop: the crop that put food on the table, paid for family living expenses throughout the year, and stood at the mercy of Mother Nature.

A wet spring could delay planting certain crops, such as cotton and corn, for weeks; a summer drought could prevent the cotton from making cotton bolls; a tornado or strong wind could destroy the cotton and corn plants or leave them flat on the ground unable to survive and mature. Excessive fall rains could delay gathering the cotton crop and decrease the quality of the picked cotton.

Rough weather struck hardest in spring and fall, and springtime was when the family especially tuned in to hear the weatherman. Whether it rained or didn't rain was crucial, and rain regularly occupied the minds of the farmers.

But what occupied the minds of us kids, especially me, was whether there'd be lightning, booming thunder, or tornadic winds mixed with the rain and threatening clouds. Thunder sometimes rattled the old windows in the house, but my greatest fear was the wind. It gained speed and ferocity as it ripped across farmland into the high hills with no obstructions to slow it before it crashed against houses and outbuildings.

We often stood in the front yard and stared up into

the black, roiling clouds that went first one way and then another. We watched mesmerized as the black clouds turned darker and more threatening as they came closer. Storm clouds in the country always seemed lower and closer to the ground than in the city. With the first flash of lightning and rumble of thunder, we made a mad dash for the house. We were afraid of storms, and this fear was intensified by Mama's constant pacing from window to window.

As refuge against storms, we had a storm house, or storm cellar as it was more commonly called. It was kept in good order, checked yearly for any sign of damage wrought through the winter. It was the main defense against inclement weather.

The storm house, common around homes in the forties and fifties, was about a hundred yards from the house. It had a wooden door and earthen walls and floor, and dirt was mounded overhead. We kept a few wooden chairs, a lantern, and some matches in the storm house. It wasn't comfortable, but it was a waiting place—a place to sit with your head on your lap and a place where watch was kept for any desperate snake that tried to enter the door to escape the storm.

A night punctuated with squall lines of spring storms gave no restful sleep. Mama and Daddy listened to the six o'clock forecast, always alert after the prediction of a big storm expected during the night. Mama lay in bed, napping while listening with one ear for the expected squall. She'd have the family up and dressed fast if a storm exceeded her tolerance.

We hated such nights and knew the house would make noises it made at no other time. We also knew that a trip to the storm house would interrupt our sleep—if we were able to sleep at all. We knew we would have to move quickly when the time came.

Once Mama and Daddy decided a storm was threatening,

we prepared to go to the storm house. Covering our heads as best we could, we followed Mama down the dirt steps with Daddy behind us to close the storm house door. Lighting the lantern, we waited as time crawled. Daddy occasionally went up the steps and raised the wooden door for a peek at the intensity of the storm. Finally a welcome quietness would fall, signaling that the storm was over, bedtime was again near, and the opportunity for rest had arrived at last.

*Chapter 8*

♣

*Christmas*

Christmas on the farm was a good time. The cotton crop had been harvested by then, and the dreaded first appearance back in the classroom was over until the next fall. By this time of year, I could attend school pretending I was just like every other student.

During my junior and senior years, I had a part-time job working Saturdays and Christmas holidays at Cohen's Department Store in Forrest City. I started out making four dollars a day waiting on customers shopping for clothes. Later my salary was raised to five dollars a day. I paid a dollar a day for my ride and saved most of my wages to help with school clothes and expenses. At that time in Arkansas, students were required to buy their own schoolbooks. My parents couldn't afford to buy that many sets of books, so the part-time job enabled me to save enough money to buy my own books.

When time came to put up the Christmas tree, my sisters and I took a hatchet and spent hours in the woods looking for *just* the right tree. Though cedar trees were scarce, Daddy sometimes gave us a hint as to where he had seen one while hunting.

We always managed to come up with some kind of tree—some prettier than others. We had one string of multi-colored electric lights, some homemade ornaments, and some icicles. Going outside at night to see the tree after it was decorated with the colorful lights remains one of my most treasured memories. The tree lights shining with the stars overhead was one of the most beautiful things I had ever seen. Even now, I decorate a small tree with the same kind of lights.

Mama's Christmas cakes, pies, and "chicken 'n' dressing" were a delight. Wearing one of her flour-sack aprons, she was busy in the kitchen for days before Christmas making fresh coconut cake, mincemeat pies, pecan pies, and chocolate pies. The mouthwatering smells emanating from the kitchen made it hard to wait for Christmas day.

Mama always made Daddy his favorite black walnut cake with walnuts we picked up in the backyard. About the size of tennis balls, the walnuts were covered with a green hull that softened and turned black after a few days in the sun. The hulls had to be removed then, and hulling the walnuts was a job we hated. Even though we wore gloves, black from the walnut husks stained our fingers for days.

The walnuts had to dry for several weeks before they were ready to shell. Once the nuts were dry we held each one against a rock or concrete block and cracked it open with a steel hammer. We all joined in shelling the walnuts and pecans at night while listening to some of our favorite radio programs like *Suspense Theater* or the *Grand Ole Opry*.

A few weeks before Christmas, Mama put a hen in the chicken coop to fatten up for the big day. The hen always had plenty of food to eat so it would be good and plump.

On the last day of school before Christmas vacation when I was in the sixth grade, my class had a Christmas party. Each girl brought a girl's gift, and each boy brought a boy's gift. A number was taped to each gift, and we drew numbers to see what gift we would get. Since we were assigned seats alphabetically, and my last name started with A, I sat at the front of the room and could see the numbers on the gifts. I was excited to see that the number I drew corresponded with the number on the largest, most beautifully wrapped gift under the Christmas tree. I couldn't wait to receive my gift.

The teacher selected Marsha, a pretty and popular classmate, to call the numbers and hand out the gifts. When Marsha called a certain number and no one immediately raised her hand to claim the gift, she came toward me with a small, unwrapped bottle of cheap perfume. "Here," she said, "you take this one." Someone else ended up with the gift that held my number.

Though Christmas presents were very modest and few in number—maybe inexpensive dolls for the girls and a toy gun for Brother Bill—the season was still a much anticipated time of the year. Treats like apples, oranges, nuts in the shell, and bags of hard candy were to be found only at Christmas. Daddy's favorite, old-fashioned chocolate drops with white cream centers surrounded by thin coatings of bittersweet chocolate, usually appeared around Christmas.

My excitement was only tempered by thoughts of returning to school after the holidays, thinking all the other kids had received lots of presents and not wanting them to know we'd barely gotten one or two small items apiece.

❧

In my junior year of high school, I attended my first girl's high school basketball game and was hooked. The competition and excitement were new experiences for me. The players wore uniforms made of a shiny white material trimmed in blue, our school colors. I thought they were beautiful. A tall girl named Jane played center position for Parkin High School, the opposing team. She had a graceful hoop shot that wowed the audience.

After seeing that game, I dreamed of playing basketball for the high school team, although I knew it would never be possible since the practices and games were held after school and I had no way of getting the ten miles home. What's more, practices began in the fall, long before I started school in November.

The following Christmas I asked Mama for a basketball and got one. It wasn't a nice basketball like the ones used at school but a rather cheap lightweight version. I knew that was all we could afford, though, and made the best of it. Next, I needed a basketball hoop.

Knowing we couldn't afford a real basketball hoop, I decided to make my own. I asked Mr. Shelton, the local blacksmith, if he could make an iron hoop. Since he was fond of me and my sisters and was aware of how hard we worked in the fields, he made the hoop at no charge.

The next step was to get a pole on which to mount the hoop. Taking Daddy's axe, Marilyn and I headed to the woods to find a tall tree. After we had chopped for what seemed like hours, the twenty-foot oak tree came crashing down. The tree hit the ground with a loud thud, but we managed to steer clear of the trunk and long limbs. After cutting and trimming the tree, Marilyn and I dragged it back to the house.

The next step was to dig a hole in the backyard for the pole. Using Daddy's post-hole digger on the packed clay dirt was hard work, but finally the hole was deep enough to support the pole.

Though the basketball goal was a little unsteady and had no net or backboard, I spent many hours dribbling and shooting basketball on my homemade court. Later, I actually attributed my dribbling ability to having to become adroit at dribbling around and avoiding chickens and chicken poop.

One day while playing basketball during gym class, I was approached by Miss Robbins, our gym teacher. "Clara, have you ever considered going out for the girl's basketball team?" she asked. I was thrilled to be asked but responded "No, ma'am," without explaining why I couldn't play on the team.

I still have a love for college basketball and football and

have had season tickets to the local university games for many years.

We were one of the last families in the New Castle community to get a television. By the time I reached the eleventh grade in 1956, only Glenda, Marilyn, and I remained at home with Mama and Daddy. We all dreamed of getting a TV since most of our friends and relatives had one. But none of us wanted one as badly as Glenda. "When we get a TV, I want to watch Dragnet," she said. She had seen the show at a friend's house and had a crush on the main actor, Jack Webb.

Since we lived in the hills, from a car you could see our house sitting on one hill as you topped another a quarter mile away. "Some day when the school bus tops that first hill, I'll see a TV antenna on top of our house," Glenda said. She had watched every afternoon for years.

One winter day in 1956, as Christmas approached, an ear-splitting scream from Glenda told everyone on the school bus that we finally had a TV! The crop had been harvested and Mama and Daddy had gone to town and bought a used console black-and-white TV. Daddy had hooked it up, antenna and all, so Glenda could see it from the bus as we were returning home from school.

When the bus stopped in front of our house to let us off, we all tore off running to see the TV. Marilyn and I were careful to let Glenda go in the house first. There, sitting in a corner of the living room, was the wonderful TV. We were too excited to eat that first night.

The program selection was limited since we had only three channels, but we thought it was fantastic even to see the news and to laugh together while watching *The Little*

*Rascals.* The TV stations signed off for the night at 10:00 P.M., but we continued to sit in front of the set that first night, watching the "pattern" on the screen until we could no longer keep our eyes open. There were smiles all around, as that was one of the happiest days of our lives.

*Chapter 9*

♣

*The Rabbit Hunt*

Farmers who couldn't afford the fertile, level delta land scratched a living out of the variable hill dirt around Crowley's Ridge. Luckily, in that area there were many ways to put food on the table. Our diets consisted mostly of vegetables raised in the garden and fish and game gathered nearby, often through hunting.

You won't often find rabbit for sale in a modern supermarket, but for the poor ridge runners (what inhabitants of the hill country around Crowley's Ridge were called), finding a platter of fried rabbit on the dinner table was a real treat. We ate front legs and back legs and pieces of back meat. The back meat was tender, but a big back leg was the most desirable. Of all the ways of acquiring food, rabbit hunting was the most fun for the hunters. Not only did it put food on the table, it was also a popular sport enjoyed by men of that era.

One of my favorite memories was getting off the school bus in late afternoon during winter months, walking in the house, and being greeted by the aroma of rabbit simmering in a large iron pot on the wood-burning heater in the living room. Daddy had been rabbit hunting, and we could look forward to a great supper with meat so tender it fell off the bone.

Rabbit hunting is done with hounds, usually beagles, but any good dog that can hold a trail will do. The dogs jump the game out of the cover of bushes and trail it until it circles back to where the hunters wait.

Daddy raised beagle hounds, and people came from miles around to buy them. The beagles, being well trained, usually brought a good price. Hearing rabbit-hunting tales told by Daddy and his buddies was a common occurrence, and we heard some stories so often that we practically had them memorized.

For example, there was the day Daddy dropped his beagle hounds, a male named Rex and a female named Lady, on a hilly plot of woods on a nearby farm called the Lincoln place, only to find some city "fella" already there training his field trial dog. Since field trial dogs walk a tighter line than other hunting dogs, the fella was irritated and claimed Daddy's dogs would mess up his field trial dog. But before anything could be settled, one of the dogs hit a trail and the three hounds were off and running.

In view of the circumstances, this brought on a feeling of intense competition as the men stood silently listening to the baying of the dogs. After a few minutes, the men saw the rabbit. They watched him make about a 110-degree turn and go up the side of a hill. Lady and the field trial dog overran the trail by several yards, but Rex was never more than two feet off the trail. He made a perfect check, and the dogs were off again.

After such a brilliant performance by Daddy's dog, the city dude could only say, "That was some kind of check." After that, all hostilities faded away, and the men enjoyed several hours of great dog running.

❧

One particular December morning arrived with the pink of dawn spreading over Crowley's Ridge in the kind of way that awakened a man to his prehistoric past. The dogs, Rex and Lady, could tell by the way Daddy and Uncle Elbert walked through the door that they were going hunting. As Daddy opened the door of the dog pen, Uncle Elbert lowered the tailgate of the pickup truck, and in a few minutes they were loaded and ready to go.

That morning they decided to hunt swamp rabbits in the L'Anguille River bottoms. Some of the swamp rabbits were as much as eighteen inches long, about twice the size of the cottontail hill rabbits. If you held a swamp rabbit by its hind legs, with its feet level with your waist, its front legs could touch the ground.

As the dogs leapt off the truck, they immediately sniffed the ground, searching for the scent of rabbit. The dogs and hunters headed for a honeysuckle thicket about thirty yards away, and by the time the hunters got there, the dogs had already jumped a rabbit. The trail was red-hot, and the dogs were raising hell. In less than a minute, a rabbit broke from the thicket and darted across an open cotton field. This made for an easy shot as Daddy raised his shotgun and ended the chase.

After the kill was made, the hunters showed the rabbit to the hounds so they would quit looking for it and get on with finding another one. But that thicket produced no more game, so the men headed closer to the river and to some big trees, dead branches, and thick undergrowth. A few minutes of kicking in the brush piles produced a big "swamper" headed through some dead tree branches that matched the rabbit's color.

Daddy could only see the critter's white tail moving in and out between the branches as the rabbit tried to put distance between itself and the hunters. Daddy knew he had to shoot fast. A glimpse of a little white tail moving at high speed forty yards away was not much of a target. But he had been shooting that Remington shotgun for many years and knew how to handle it.

A blast from that old 12-gauge stopped the rabbit in the middle of a big pile of branches. This made the rabbit hard to retrieve, and the hunters knew they had to get there before the hounds; the dogs would eat a rabbit and leave only a few pieces of fur on the ground if given the chance—no head, no feet, just fur.

This made two for Daddy, none for Uncle Elbert. That didn't mean Daddy was the better hunter; it was just the luck of the draw. But there was always friendly competition among hunters to see who could get the most game.

The two hunters walked along the river bottoms with the hounds in front of them for about a hundred yards when the dogs got excited again, their tails wagging vigorously. When this happened, Daddy knew a rabbit had been through the area recently; but he couldn't tell how long ago it had been, so he paid close attention to the dogs. He knew that when the trail got hot enough, the dogs would bark. This trail got that hot, and the dogs were off. The deep, prolonged tones of baying hounds are like a symphony to hunters, and both man and dog enjoy the chase.

The dogs ran the rabbit so far up the river bottoms that Daddy and Uncle Elbert could barely hear them. Then the music started getting louder, and the hunters knew the action was headed their way. As the dogs got within about a hundred yards of the hunters, they knew the rabbit was close. The most exciting part of the hunt had arrived.

The challenge was to stand quiet and not spook the game as it moved through the cover. Daddy saw the rabbit off to his right, but by the time he raised his gun, the critter had disappeared into a cane thicket. The hounds followed as the rabbit got out of shooting distance, not an uncommon occurrence. The hunters would simply wait for the hounds to bring him around again. This time the rabbit almost ran over Uncle Elbert, and when Daddy heard the shotgun blast, he knew the chase was over.

As the men hunted on up the river bottoms, they came to a honeysuckle patch that bordered the woods on one side and an open cotton field on the other. They knew it was very likely the thicket contained what they wanted, so the men separated, one on each side. The hounds jumped a rabbit in the honeysuckle, and the rabbit ran into the cotton field where Daddy was waiting. With the animal being visible only between the cotton stalks, Daddy made a successful long shot at fifty yards. The men collected their prize and went on across the field. By the end of the day, Daddy had five rabbits, and Uncle Elbert had three—a good day of hunting.

⌘

Rabbit hunting, like deer and squirrel hunting, is legal only during certain months of the year. During the off-season, when it was illegal to hunt game, it was still within the law to run rabbit dogs. Daddy enjoyed exercising his dogs, and it kept them in shape.

One spring Sunday morning, just as the crocuses and buttercups were beginning to surface after a long winter, Daddy wanted to run the dogs. Not accustomed to attending church and rationalizing that God was in the outdoors just the same as He was in the small, white frame church building that sat on concrete blocks just a stone's throw from the house, Daddy didn't give a second thought to not being in church. Of course, Mama was in her usual pew at the church as she was most every Sunday.

As soon as Daddy turned the dogs loose, they picked up on a rabbit trail leading directly to the church. As the dogs neared the church, the baying sounds distracted the worshipers. The preacher and the congregation just ignored them and tried to concentrate on his sermon from the book of Revelation. Just as the preacher spoke about chapter 8, verse 6, in which the seven angels are readying to blow their trumpets, the hounds ran a rabbit under the church.

As the hounds bayed right under the church, some of the more devout members were sure they were hearing the angel's trumpets. Fearing that Judgment Day was at hand, some bowed their heads, praying for mercy and saying amens. The preacher was amazed. In all his days of spreading the Word, he had never seen so many heads bowed with lips moving, praying for repentance.

As the dogs followed the trail out from under the church and on across the parking lot, the preacher and some of the elders assured the congregation that the noise had just been barking dogs and they would have to wait a little longer to see the angels.

Mama was terribly embarrassed, knowing all the while it was Daddy and his dogs doing the misdeed. When Daddy picked her up after church, Mama gave him her strongest expression of disapproval: "*The very idea!*"

*Chapter 10*

♣

*Elaine Massacre*

The race riot called the Elaine Massacre occurred in October 1919 in Elaine, Arkansas, between black sharecroppers and white landowners. In one of the greatest injustices of our time involving events that have been largely overlooked by history books, whites rioted against the black population.

As with many racial histories of this kind, it was one of those shameful events that were "not talked about," but it is also a story that has to be told. It is a part of our history. And just like we don't need to forget about 9/11, Pearl Harbor, and the Civil War, these stories need to be told.

The untimely death of my great uncle, on Daddy's side of the family, ignited the deadly riot and ensuing massacre. Daddy was an eleven-year-old child when his uncle, William Adkins, was shot and killed by black sharecroppers in nearby Elaine. As a child growing up, I always wondered why Daddy had a racist attitude. Though inexcusable, the following events may have contributed to his feelings toward black folk.

❧

Phillips County, Arkansas, encompasses the small towns of Helena and Elaine. Phillips County is approximately thirty miles from St. Francis County, Arkansas, where I grew up. Though these events happened many years before I was born, I have been able, through family memories and research, to reconstruct much of the history of the shameful events that took place during that time.

For many years, the white landowners in Phillips County, predominately a farming community, had been taking advantage of the black tenant farmers—cheating them out of their fair share of the cotton crops they raised on the landowners' properties. In order to support their families until the crops sold, the sharecroppers arranged credit with the planters at local general stores, often owned or controlled by the landlords themselves.

In many stores, sharecroppers were not only charged prices that were much higher than normal for what they bought, but they also were charged usurious rates of interest. Many black sharecroppers worked for years without seeing a penny, finding themselves ever deeper in debt—often because the landlords kept the books. Some of the sharecroppers were charged for items they never purchased. It was not unusual for a landlord to give a sharecropper a piece of paper with "balance due" written on it but with no itemized statement of actual expenses. If a black farmer protested the charge, he would be driven off the farm, sometimes beaten or even killed.

Black sharecroppers were even discouraged by the landowners from raising their own gardens and meat. Landowners sought to minimize the amount of food the sharecroppers produced on their own, making the sharecroppers more dependent on landowners for food; this was one way of keeping the sharecroppers in debt. The landowners insisted that cotton be planted right up to the cabin with little or no yard left, minimizing the useful space for gardens.

White sharecroppers who dreamed of becoming landowners found they could neither buy nor rent land. Large planters found it cheaper to rent their land to black farmers whom they knew they could exploit without fear of legal retaliation.

By 1919 very few blacks owned farms in Phillips County. They had been drafted into the army during World War I where their military service had awakened a dormant resentment of the second-class citizenship they had been given. They struggled to gain some semblance of equality in the country that had sent them into battle.

As part of a protest movement sweeping America, a number of black farmers in Phillips County, some of whom were veterans, decided to take a stand. They formed a union called the Progressive Farmers and Household Union. Whites later charged that the blacks were planning an insurrection against whites. Fearful whites spread rumors that blacks were storing arms and ammunition and planning an assault on the white community. Though the rumors were questionable, the grounds for this charge lay in the fact that in rural Arkansas any union of black sharecroppers dedicated to obtaining equal treatment with whites was viewed by the white landowners as an insurrection.

Rumors that blacks were organizing a union encouraged white leaders to form a committee to investigate the matter. One of the county's prominent merchants hired a private investigator from Chicago to look into the black group's intentions. Reports suggested that black sharecroppers and tenant farmers had organized a union and were plotting the assassination of several white planters. According to the investigator, the murders were to take place in early October in Elaine, a small Arkansas community consisting predominately of black sharecroppers and tenant farmers.

Blacks claimed they were denied the right to make cash settlements for their crops, were unable to turn to legal means for assistance, and were not allowed to move from the land to improve conditions. In 1919, U. S. Bratton, a former attorney general, reported that one black tenant farmer in Elaine had been shot and permanently crippled by his landlord because he asked for a cash settlement for his crop.

As a result of the conflict in Europe during World War I, the price of cotton rose, and black sharecroppers in Phillips

County became more insistent on claiming their rightful share of their cotton crops. Black farmers in surrounding counties also felt they had been cheated out of what was due them from the 1918 harvest; so they were determined things would be different in 1919.

Sixty-eight of the black sharecroppers got together and decided to hire a lawyer to get statements of their accounts and a settlement of the right figures. They found that the white Little Rock firm of Bratton and Bratton was a good, reliable firm and would fight for any client to the last. Some of the black farmers also planned to go before the federal grand jury and charge some of the white planters who had cheated them with peonage.

*Peonage* is defined as holding a person in servitude to a creditor until a debt is satisfied. Landowners in Phillips County advanced sharecroppers small amounts of money to recruit them to their plantations; then the sharecroppers would not be allowed to leave until their indebtedness was satisfied. Since the landowners kept the books, they could ensure that these debts would never be paid.

The black sharecroppers met from time to time to collect money, discuss evidence, and gather facts that would enable them to successfully prosecute these cases. These meetings had to be secret to prevent harm to the men concerned and to their families.

On the night of September 30, 1919, a group of black farmers met at a church in a place called Hoop Spur, a railroad junction not far from the town of Elaine. As the farmers met in the church, a car drove up carrying two law enforcement officials. One of them was my Uncle Will Adkins, a special agent for the Missouri Pacific Railroad, who also served as the local sheriff. The other was Charles Pratt, a local deputy sheriff. Saying what happened next depends on which version of the tale you believe.

Uncle Will, with Pratt riding in the passenger seat beside him, stopped the car beside the Hoop Spur Church. Later, town officials claimed that the law enforcement officers were looking for a bootlegger and were at the church by mistake. Others claimed the officials had planned to break up the meeting. Whatever the reality, a confrontation developed between the officers and the blacks. Uncle Will was shot and killed, and Pratt was seriously wounded.

Another version has it that the white men stopped and attempted to investigate the meeting. They were refused admittance to the church, so they tried to break in and fired into the building. Some blacks inside the church returned the fire, killing Uncle Will and injuring Pratt.

Later, all mention of the white men was carefully avoided and suppressed, and the entire blame was laid upon the blacks at the church. Law officials claimed all the blacks were armed and that the white men were proceeding peaceably on the road and had only gotten out to fix their car, which just happened to break down right in front of this particular church. According to this version, the blacks fired on the two men without any provocation.

Uncle Will's death sparked racial fires that smoldered for decades to come. The parish sheriff called for a posse to investigate and capture those responsible for the killing. Violence expanded beyond the meeting place.

Armed white men poured into the county from outside to support the white citizens until a mob of between five hundred and a thousand armed men had formed. The cry of "Negro uprising! Negro insurrection!" went out. The white planters called their gangs together, and a big "Negro hunt" began. The white planters rushed their women and children to the nearby town of Helena.

Carloads and trains full of white men, armed to the teeth, came from Marianna and Forrest City, Arkansas,

Clarksdale, Mississippi, and Memphis, Tennessee. Rifles and ammunition were rushed in. The woods were scoured and black homes shot into. Blacks who didn't know any trouble was brewing were shot and killed on the highways.

A crowd of enraged men splashed across the shallows of the river, with, as historian Robert Whitaker puts it, "blood in their eyes." Whitaker goes on: "They shot and killed men, women and children without regard to whether they were guilty or innocent of any connection with the killing of anybody, or whether members of the union or not. Blacks were killed time and time again out in the fields picking cotton, harming nobody."

Blacks who collected the bodies did so anonymously; no reporter came to ask them what they found. An ex-soldier who lived nearby wrote in a letter to Howard University: "It was a good many of Negroes down their [sic] killed and the white Peoples [sic] called for the troops from Little Rock and they went down their [sic] and killed Negroes like they wont nothen [sic] but dogs."

The picture Whitaker portrays is as accurate a description of that day as any, and as Henry Smiddy, another Missouri Pacific Special Agent, headed back to Helena that Thursday night, his thoughts were no different. He passed the church in Hoop Spur where it had all started and saw that it had been burned.

He had been at a place called Govan Slough, just outside Helena, and had spent all of Thursday in the field with the posses. The scenes of the many killing fields, amounting to a massacre, ultimately all ran together. "I do not know how many Negroes were killed in all," he said later, "but I do know that there were between two and three hundred Negroes killed that I saw with my own eyes."

Many times, my mother related stories about the terrible treatment of blacks during the uprising, how they were hunted down in the fields and shot. One of the saddest stories relayed was about the killing of the four Johnston brothers.

The Johnston brothers were sons of a prominent local black Presbyterian minister. The four brothers had gone squirrel hunting early in the morning on the first day of the trouble and started for home in the afternoon, not knowing about the events at Hoop Spur. While they were miles out in the woods hunting, word of the trouble reached Helena. A merchant told the deputy sheriff and posse that he had sold some shells to the Johnstons a day or so before.

A crowd of men in a car went to look for the Johnstons and met them returning from the hunt. The white men were supposed to be friends of the brothers. They told them about the trouble, that a riot was in progress, and that it would be dangerous for a black person to be on the country roads, especially with a gun. The Johnstons told them they had just been hunting and had nothing but shotguns and squirrel shot. They were advised by their "friends" to turn back and go home by a train that would pass a little station several miles down the road. They took this advice and went to the station to go by train to Helena.

The four brothers had bought their tickets and boarded the train when a car rolled up with some deputies. They arrested three of the men and took them from the train. The fourth brother, a doctor from Oklahoma, also got off. When Dr. Johnston got off the train, the officers told him to get back on. He refused, saying, "These men are my brothers. If you arrest them, I will go too." The officers said, "Well, if you are one of the Johnston brothers, we want you too." They then arrested the Oklahoma man, whose only crime was being the brother of the other three, whose crime was equally unclear.

The men were loaded into a car and traveled back down

the same road they had come over. After a few miles, a crowd of white men appeared, led by the very same white "friends" who had warned the Johnstons to take the train. They had sent word to the officers about where they could get the Johnstons. At this point the Johnston brothers could see that they had been led into a trap. Although they were handcuffed, they tried to put up a fight. Just as one of the officers climbed out of the car, preparing to turn the helpless men over to the mob, Dr. Johnston, though shackled, managed to grab the officer's pistol from his hand and shot him. The officers and the mob then shot the men literally to pieces. They were shot with so many bullets that their faces had to be covered at the funeral and parts of their bodies were in shreds.

Telegrams were sent from the Elaine mayor to Arkansas Governor Charles Brough: "Race riots here in Elaine and we need some soldiers at once. Several white men and Negroes killed last night and this morning." Governor Brough called for federal troops, and five hundred were rushed from Camp Pike, armed with rifles, gas masks, hand grenades, bombs, machine guns, and artillery. The colonel took charge and mobilized his men to "repel the attack of the black army." The country was scoured for a radius of fifty to a hundred miles, covering all of Phillips and parts of adjoining counties for "Negro insurrectionists."

Colonel Isaac Jenks, commander of the Camp Pike troops, thought the situation was as bad as Brough had said: the whites in Elaine were surrounded, and out on the farms, blacks were indiscriminately shooting whites. Colonel Jenks, an imposing figure dressed in officer's uniform, led the troops, numbering more than four hundred, as they began their march "to kill any Negro who refuses to surrender immediately."

The remainder of the troops headed west behind a posse.

They had been advised about 150 blacks hiding in the woods and canebrake west of town and in the Yellow Banks Bayou east of Route 44. The troops had been ordered to *shoot to kill* at the first sign of resistance. As they approached the canebrake, a shot rang out and grazed one of the troops. The soldiers responded with rapid machine gun and rifle fire.

According to Governor Brough, "They took machine guns out there and let 'em have it." A soldier was later heard to say, "They were shooting them down like rabbits." However, a reporter with the *Memphis Press* who was following the troops indicated that "hardly any of the blacks had guns or ammunition."

Frank Moore, a strong black man, five feet, eight inches tall, had been discharged from the U.S. Army the previous December. He and his father had planted fifty acres of cotton that spring and were excited to hear cotton could bring as much as fifty cents a pound that fall. Moore joined the union thinking it could finally be the year he would get his fair share of his cotton crop. But that was before October 1 and Hoop Spur.

As night fell on October 2, after a day of killing, Moore and his family hunkered down in the tall canebrake along with hundreds of other men, women, and children. They left their cabins looking for a safe place to hide. The thick river cane, fifteen to twenty feet tall, provided a safe haven for the night, but the sharecroppers knew that when daylight came the hunt would be on again.

The next morning, Frank Moore and the others crept to the edge of the canebrake where they had spent the night. As they stepped out, they saw the army troops coming up the road. The troops captured Moore and the other families and jailed them in an old white schoolhouse.

Lambrook Plantation was located in the community of Lambrook, a few miles west of Elaine. Gerard Lambert, owner of Lambrook Plantation, had over seven hundred black sharecroppers working for him. When the squad of Camp Pike soldiers reached Lambrook Plantation, they immediately rounded up one of the supposed black ringleaders. In his autobiography, *All Out of Step,* Gerard Lambert writes of the incident:

> Troopers brought him to our company store and tied him with stout cord to one of the wooden columns on the outer porch. He had been extremely insolent, and the troopers, enraged by the loss of two of their men that day in the woods, had pressed him with questions. He continued his arrogance, and one white man, hoping to make him speak up, poured a can of kerosene over him. As he was clearly unwilling to talk, a man suddenly tossed a lighted match at him. The colored man went up like a torch and, in a moment of supreme agony, burst his bounds. Before he could get but a few feet he was riddled with bullets.

That same afternoon, the soldiers began a search of the sharecropper's cabins and recovered four hundred guns and two hundred pistols. This was not surprising—it was not unusual for sharecroppers or farmers to own guns—but what began as a search turned into another day of killing. Sharpe Dunaway, a well-known Arkansas newspaperman wrote in 1925:

> The thing that "stumps" us, however, is by what authority did a coterie of federal

soldiers, aided and abetted by a collection of low-lived creatures who call themselves *White Men,* march down among the ramshackle homes of good old innocent, hard-working Darkeys [*sic*], and then and there unlimber their guns on those poor old servants of the rebellion, finally snuffing out their lives before passing on to the next house, where the same cruel scene was enacted, thus leaving a path strewn with aching hearts and besprinkled with the red blood of innocent humanity.

The soldiers, Dunaway concluded, "committed one murder after another with all the calm and deliberation in the world."

Ed Coleman, who stayed in the woods that morning, crept back to his cabin later that afternoon. When he got there, he found that "the white men had shot and killed some of the women and children." Coleman felt, however, that the killings might have been committed by the posses who were there ahead of the soldiers.

According to Coleman, there was evidence some of the soldiers tried to help the wounded sharecroppers. They dressed the bullet wounds of one of the men and took him to the hospital; the soldiers also cared for the man's brother. According to Dunaway, there was at least that touch of humanity, and so it may simply be that with the troops moving across a cotton field two miles wide, there were instances that afternoon of both "bloodthirsty" murder and of decency.

**Hoop Spur Church, site of Uncle Will's death**

౮ఎ

The total number of blacks killed in the uprising has never been determined, but documentation exists for twenty-two killing sites. It is not known how many blacks were slaughtered in the largest killing fields, where hundreds hid surrounded by troops.

What many people remembered about the tragic events were the number of black corpses lying everywhere—in the fields, on the roadsides, and around the sharecroppers' cabins. The dead bodies were left for a few days before they were buried; this was done to show the other blacks what would happen if they tried to assert themselves again.

Dunaway wrote, "The stench of dead bodies could be smelled for miles."

The black farmers had dreamed of simply getting their fair share of the cotton crop; and now more than a hundred were dead, and three hundred were in jail. The union had been abolished, and many of those who survived were looking at possible death sentences.

The first published reports of the tragic events in Phillips County were dated October 2, 1919, by the Associated Press and Arkansas newspapers. Telephone and telegraph lines were immediately cut from Elaine and Hoop Spur, which meant that, going forward, the flow of information to the media was controlled by officials in Helena.

The papers said when Helena posses drove out to arrest the blacks who had "murdered" Adkins, they were met by a "group of armed Negroes" with high-powered rifles who began firing on white persons. The blacks were said to greatly outnumber the whites. Another newspaper account told of blacks doing the unthinkable, waging a "war" on whites. "They had killed Adkins and two others for no reason, and they had nearly killed the governor too," one paper reported.

Outrageous newspaper stories continued as the so-called Committee of Seven declared that the union had been formed by blacks for the purpose of killing white people. The Committee of Seven, appointed by Governor Brough, was composed of seven of the town's "leading businessmen" to investigate the Negro revolt and decide who should be prosecuted. The committee also claimed black farmers were building large warehouses to house enormous supplies of arms and ammunition they were collecting.

According to the newspapers, this was what the sharecroppers had been planning when Uncle Will was killed at the church at Hoop Spur. Uncle Will and the three other whites who died were eulogized as heroes who had died in the line of duty. Governor Brough's voice cracked as he told Little Rock reporters, "The County has lost some of its most prominent and promising citizens."

As the shooting quieted during the second week of October, the citizens' committee posted circulars throughout town telling blacks to go back to work in the cotton fields and that the Elaine "insurrection" was over. Most of the women were released from jail.

When the women who belonged to the union returned to their homes, they found everything gone: chickens, hogs, household goods, and clothes had all been taken away or burned. At the beginning of the year they had had high hopes of making a profit that year with the price of cotton so high, but now the Hoop Spur women and children were penniless and starving.

The soldiers had arrested over a thousand blacks, men and women, and placed them in a stockade under heavy guard and in harsh, unsanitary conditions. They were not allowed to see friends or attorneys, but all of them had to be separately and personally "investigated" by the army officers and the white "Committee of Seven."

The Phillips County jail cells overflowed with black Hoop Spur sharecroppers to the point that Helena authorities moved some prisoners to a makeshift jail in a nearby warehouse. All the so-called union leaders, however, were kept in jail at the courthouse, and they soon found out why.

As the Committee of Seven began their interrogations, the sharecroppers refused to lie and tell the committee what it wanted to hear. When committee members tried to put words in the sharecroppers' mouths, the farmers would say they didn't know or answer, "No, sir." If a sharecropper refused to lie about himself or another one of the prisoners, he would be taken to another room at the jail for a torture session.

William Wordlow, one of the prisoners, had to testify against some of the other men. When he told the committee, "I don't know anything to tell against these men," he was stripped and whipped with a rubber strap that was embedded with metal. Wordlow said, "Every lick would cut the blood out." Wordlow said the other blacks were often tortured the same way. The officers would tell him to say certain things or they would kill him.

At the end of the whippings, if the officers were not satisfied, they picked the bleeding men up and put them in a chair that had been rigged like an electric chair. The current was turned on and increased until the men couldn't tolerate the pain. After such a torture session, the prisoner was usually unable to walk back to his cell and had to be dragged.

According to T. K. Jones, one of the officials, a number of the prisoners had to be whipped two or three times before they would agree to give false testimony. On second or third whippings, the leather strap reopened old sores and usually got the black man to say whatever he was told if he had refused the first time.

Frank Moore, one of the tortured prisoners, refused to break. Moore said, "I was whipped nearly to death to make me tell stories on others, to say we killed the white people, when at the church that night I didn't have a gun whatever." He stated, "I would rather die than to tell something on myself or others that was not true."

On November 3, 1919, trials for the accused began. The prosecution's case was this: the sharecroppers had formed the Progressive and Farmer's Union in order "to kill planters," but the insurrection had erupted prematurely when Adkins was gunned down. The defendants, never having spoken to their defense attorneys, were not aware they had been charged with first-degree murder.

As their trial began, a mob surrounded the courthouse, threatening to lynch the defendants if they were not sentenced to death. The defendants were denied the right to meet with counsel before trial. Charges were made against them; false confessions were used in evidence; and the jury deliberated just minutes per defendant before finding each guilty.

On November 4, 1919, Alf Banks Jr. and John Martin, two of the guards outside the church at Hoop Spur, were convicted of the murder of Uncle Will. Out for only nine minutes, the jury returned a guilty verdict. The penalty was death.

Also on November 4, the jury convicted William Wordlow, another guard outside the church, of aiding and abetting in the death of Uncle Will. The jury was out two minutes: another death penalty.

In the end, the judge sentenced all twelve men to death.

But the case was far from closed. Scipio Africanus Jones, a successful African American attorney in Little Rock, decided he would try to mobilize support to save the lives of the condemned men.

Born to a slave (his father was likely his mother's owner), Jones became the most prominent black lawyer in Little Rock. Unknown to Jones, the NAACP had also decided to appeal the death sentences. Walter White, executive secretary of the NAACP, had hired Colonel George Murphy, a well-known white attorney from Little Rock, to take on the case.

Jones and Murphy eventually worked together on behalf of the condemned men. The lawyers agreed their strongest argument was that the defendants did not have a fair trial because of the presence of the mob outside the courthouse and because the confessions of some of the witnesses had been obtained though torture. Using this argument, Jones and Murphy were twice able to win new trials for six of the condemned men. But in each case, the men were again sentenced to death.

Murphy died shortly after the second trial and was replaced by his partner Edgar McHaney. Meanwhile, the other six defendants who had been denied new trials were only hours away from execution. The only chance they had was to have their case reviewed by the U. S. Supreme Court. Jones and McHaney were successful in obtaining a stay for the defendants but didn't know for how long.

By then Jones was working with NAACP lawyer Moorefield Storey. Storey feared the U.S. Supreme Court would reject their argument that the men were denied a fair trial because of the mob; in 1913 the Supreme Court had rejected that argument in the Leo Frank case.

Leo Frank was a Jewish factory manager in Georgia. When a 16-year-old girl who worked in the factory was murdered, Frank was falsely accused of the crime. A mob surrounded the Georgia courthouse demanding his death. The judge and jury complied, and the Georgia courts upheld the decision. The Supreme Court refused to intervene, and Frank was eventually taken out of prison by a mob and lynched.

In the Elaine case, Jones and Storey felt that the main hope for the Court to reverse itself was Justice Oliver Wendell Holmes, who had disagreed with the majority of his colleagues in the Frank case. Their hope was rewarded in 1923 when the Supreme Court ordered the case back to the federal district courts for further review.

Holmes wrote the majority opinion (*Moore vs. Dempsey*, 1923) invoking the Fourteenth Amendment to the U.S. Constitution and affirming that the twelve men were convicted in a "kangaroo trial" and denied due process of law. This decision saved their lives. For the first time in American history, black defendants gained legal rights in criminal cases.

By then public opinion in Arkansas had shifted in favor of the condemned men, who, along with everyone else who was still in prison after being arrested during the incident, were released.

In the 1940s and 1950s, the federal government's agricultural policies, such as paying planters not to grow cotton, weakened the sharecropper system. During World War II, many blacks migrated north, and others joined the armed forces. After the war, cotton picking machines were introduced into the fields, making hand labor obsolete. By the 1960s, sharecropping, long dying, was virtually dead.

Though some local white residents of Phillips County still contend that white people at the time acted appropriately to prevent a slaughter in the Elaine area in 1919, the modern view of most historians of this crisis is that white mobs unjustifiably killed an undetermined number of African Americans. More controversial is the view that the military participated in the murder of blacks. Race relations in this area of Arkansas remained strained for decades for a number of reasons, including the events of 1919.

# Chapter 11

♣

*Forrest City*

Forrest City, Arkansas, was named as a result of General Nathan Bedford Forrest using the location as a campsite for a construction crew soon after the Civil War. Forrest, the famous Confederate general, became interested in the area around Crowley's Ridge. An intriguing character, he became head of his family at the tender age of seventeen. He managed to raise his family out of poverty to become one of the South's richest men in pre-war Memphis.

First a farmer and then a plantation owner, Forrest was a slave trader on Front Street in Memphis by the time the Civil War started. At its peak, Memphis was the largest inland cotton market in the United States. But cotton wasn't the only booming business; the slave market was booming as well. Forrest was one of a group of businessmen who opened slave showrooms on Front Street. Said to have kept his business fair and his slave pens clean, Forrest prospered as one of the South's largest slave traders, selling up to one thousand slaves per year.

Forrest took up arms during the Civil War and, in spite of near illiteracy, rose in rank to become one of the greatest military tacticians in American history. His surprise attacks on Union troops in Memphis would later inspire the German blitzkrieg. During the war, he became a legendary rebel, Confederate general, and perhaps the American Civil War's most highly regarded cavalry soldier and ranger.

Regarded by many military historians as the war's most innovative and successful general, Forrest's tactics of mobile warfare are still studied by modern soldiers. Locally, in one humiliating raid, his band stormed and temporarily freed Union-occupied Memphis; in another, he stole the occupying Union general's uniform from his bedroom while he slept.

In modern times, Forrest's reputation suffers not only

because of the stain of being a slave trader but also due to his involvement in the early Ku Klux Klan following the war. Forrest later called for the disbanding of the Klan and distanced himself from it. In 1875 he was invited as the first Anglo American man to speak before a forerunner organization of the NAACP, where he declared his belief in the peaceful inclusion of African Americans in public life. However, his early slave trading and his involvement in the start-up of the Klan still create controversy and carry a stigma.

After the Civil War, Forrest became president of the Marion and Memphis Railroad and established a camp at the present site of Forrest City. Afterward he contracted with railroad companies in Memphis and Little Rock to cut through the rough ridge and succeeded in linking Memphis and Little Rock by rail in 1868.

General Forrest later built a commissary located on Front Street, and Colonel V. B. Izard began the task of designing the town. Most citizens were calling the area "Forrest's Town," thus evolved the name Forrest City.

Forrest City, with a population of about twelve thousand, is located on Crowley's Ridge, a geological feature that rises above the flat delta land that surrounds it. It is a combination of rolling hills, flatland, woods, and creek bottoms.

This north-to-south ridge is about three miles wide and rises some three hundred feet above the surrounding land, having its northern termination in the hilly region northwest of Cape Girardeau, Missouri, and running in a southerly direction, inclining a little east between the St. Francis and White rivers for about 250 miles, and terminating in a bluff at Helena, Arkansas.

Several species of trees not indigenous to Arkansas are found here, including beech, butternut, sugar maple, and cucumber trees. Crowley's Ridge provides some of the most beautiful scenery in eastern Arkansas, especially in the fall when changing leaf colors are at their peak. In the spring the ridge comes alive with flowering dogwood and redbud blooms.

Proof that giant mastodons roamed the slope was uncovered in 1949 when workmen excavating sewer lines found fossils of the massive beast within the limits of Forrest City. The American mastodon, which became extinct about ten thousand years ago, closely resembled today's elephants. The mastodon was slightly shorter than an elephant but more heavily built, weighing four to six tons. They were eight to ten feet tall at the shoulder and had long, reddish-brown hair. Mastodon's lived in the area along Crowley's Ridge and the Mississippi River, inhabiting woody or swampy areas. A few mastodon skeletons were even found with the fur still attached.

Native American pottery and prehistoric artifacts have been found on Crowley's Ridge in more recent years. Numerous pieces of pottery and weapons, such as tomahawks, arrowheads, and spears, were uncovered and are currently on display at the St. Francis County Museum in Forrest City.

❧

Typical of small towns in the South, Forrest City had two movie theaters, the Imperial Theater in the downtown area and the Sky-Vue Drive-In on the outskirts of town. The drive-in was an inexpensive place to take the whole family to the movies. I remember lighting little curly green things that produced fumes meant to keep the mosquitoes away; I couldn't tell that they had much effect, though.

I'm just old enough to remember the "colored" balcony at the Imperial Theater. Marilyn, Glenda, and I saw our first

Elvis movie, *Love Me Tender* there. The movie starred Elvis Presley, Richard Egan, and Debra Paget. Other popular celebrities during the fifties were Sandra Dee, Annette Funicello, Troy Donahue, Rock Hudson, and Doris Day; however, the biggest draws were Western movies starring Roy Rogers and Gene Autry.

The most impressive building in Forrest City was the St. Francis County Courthouse. It was a fabulous old building with huge clocks mounted on all four sides of the pointed steeple. None of the clocks ever worked during my lifetime.

Inside the courthouse was a wide, dark hallway with double doors at either end that let in light. The floor was old, worn wood, and a wooden staircase led to the second floor. A rickety wooden bridge that went over the railroad tracks led to the courthouse. If you didn't want to drive over the scary bridge, you could park on the street and mount the endless steps leading to the front entrance. The old courthouse wasn't pretty, but it had great character.

ల

Forrest City was a quiet town with little excitement or publicity, but as in many small towns, Forrest City had its share of political corruption.

There was the case of the local sheriff, Coolidge Conlee, who ran an illegal car-theft ring and was later convicted of extortion, racketeering, and drug dealing. Conlee died in 1990 while serving a twenty-year federal prison sentence. His involvement in the case of Wayne Dumond, who was convicted of the rape of a Forrest City teenager, made national news. The victim was the daughter of a prominent Forrest City mortician.

In May 1985 while free on bond and awaiting trial on

the rape charges, Wayne Dumond was savagely attacked when two masked men, armed with a handgun, razor blade, and fishing wire, broke into his Forrest City home. They hogtied him and then castrated him with the fishing wire and razor blade. Dumond's two sons found him not long after. He had lost an enormous amount of blood and was barely alive when he was rushed to the hospital; however, he managed to survive the attack.

The idea arose that Conlee might have been behind the castration when he scooped up Dumond's testicles, put them in a fruit jar filled with formaldehyde, and displayed them on his desk with this warning: "That's what happens to people who fool around in my county." Conlee was also a friend of the rape victim's father. Neither of the men who castrated Dumond was ever arrested. Dumond was later found guilty of rape and sentenced to life in prison.

Despite the usual petty criminal element found in small towns, Forrest City still had some of that ingrained "Mayberry" quality that I became more aware of on visits home after leaving for college.

As in many rural areas, proper pronunciation of certain words and places was often considered "citified." First-time visitors to Forrest City were sometimes surprised at the correct spelling of the city's name since most locals referred to it simply as "Far City."

☙

Growing up around Forrest City, I often dreamed of living in a white-painted house. Our houses had all been gray, weathered, unpainted ones belonging to the landowners whose land we farmed. When one of Mama's elderly uncles passed away, his house and small farm were put up for sale.

The neat white house was in the center of the New Castle Community.

We immediately begged Daddy to buy the house and farm, but he was reluctant to do so since he didn't feel he could afford it. Actually his reluctance stemmed from the fact that he would have to get a loan to buy the place; he believed strongly in "paying as you go" and didn't want to be in debt. Finally, after encouragement from some highly respected members of the community, he was persuaded to buy the house and land. We were thrilled.

The white house was in the middle of the community, closer to neighbors than we had been before. It was also within walking distance of the church we attended. The house sat in the middle of a lovely tree-filled lot and was much nicer than any place we had lived. We still didn't have an indoor bathroom, though, until one was added to the house years later.

I loved that house. Riding the school bus into the city each day, I had silently chosen houses that I dreamed of living in. They were not fancy, but they were always white; white houses symbolized many things that I had dreamed of but that had always seemed out of reach. This house was one of the homes I had chosen.

Although most of my growing-up years were spent in the house where I was born, the white house and land became officially known as the Adkins Home Place, where my parents lived until their deaths. Over the years, after we were grown and had families of our own, we had many happy family gatherings there. The house still stands today. When visiting the area, I usually drive by to look lovingly at the home place.

**Mastodon bones uncovered on Crowley's Ridge in 1949**
*Courtesy of St. Francis County Museum*

**Forrest City Courthouse**

**Adkins Home Place as seen today**

*Chapter 12*

♣

*College*

In the spring of 1957, as my senior year was coming to a close and graduation drew near, I applied to Draughon's Business College in nearby Memphis, Tennessee. Since money was not available for tuition, I paid a visit to Planters Bank and Trust Company in Forrest City to discuss the possibility of obtaining a loan. When the loan officer explained I needed collateral to obtain a loan, I went home and looked up *collateral* in the dictionary.

Having no collateral, I asked Mr. Earl Horton, a neighbor and member of a prominent local family, to cosign a loan at the bank. Mr. Earl, as we called him, kindly consented to help. Though this was not what I had dreamed of doing, I was excited to begin the next chapter of my life. At my high school graduation, I received several honors including the scholarship I had earned but would be unable to use.

Feeling guilty about leaving the farm work for the rest of the family, I helped with the cotton chopping the summer before leaving for college. My going away to school would leave only Marilyn and Glenda at home to help Mama and Daddy with the cotton crop.

Saying good-bye to my family and friends was sentimental, but I was ready to move on—and leave the hard work on the farm. I had plans to make a better life for myself.

I can only imagine the dreadful thoughts Mama and Daddy must have had at the prospect of my leaving and eventually Marilyn and Glenda, the last two kids, leaving home to make their own lives. They would be left without any means of making a living and with no help from their kids, very little money, sickness and old age coming on, and the loneliness of being left with just the two of them in the house. But they never even hinted at such a look into the future for themselves.

I enrolled in college in the fall of 1957 and was fortunate to get a part-time job working in the office at a local Sears store. This helped with expenses for room and board at the local YWCA, where I lived cheaply. I took most of my courses in the mornings and worked at Sears Broad Street Annex in the afternoons. Sears Annex was where catalog orders were filled and goods loaded on trucks going to catalog outlets in surrounding towns. My job was to type the bills of lading that listed the items to be loaded on each truck. It was a good part-time job that I enjoyed.

I walked the five blocks to school each morning and rode a city bus from school to work in the afternoon. It was often dark by the time I left work for the bus ride home. I was dropped off at a bus stop about two blocks from the Y but was never afraid of the dark walk home since crime was practically nonexistent at the time.

Studying late each night, I always came to class prepared. Good grades were very important to me. The highlight of my college years, other than having a 4.0 GPA, was being nominated for Prettiest Girl in the annual "Who's Who" contest. Although I didn't win, the nomination was a huge surprise and boost to my self-confidence. I had always been quite sure I wasn't pretty, and growing up among my sisters confirmed my belief. Maxine and Marilyn had both participated in beauty contests, and Glenda was selected the cutest girl in her class in high school.

It was during this time that I started dating for real. Enjoying the attention from boys and the excitement of having dates, I (along with my beaus) attended events like the Mid South Fair in the fall and the Memphis Cotton Carnival in the spring.

The Cotton Carnival was held right on the banks of the Mississippi River in downtown Memphis. Huge crowds attended the carnival, and we were dazzled by all that was going on simultaneously: exhibits, people in costumes, carnival rides, and various performances. People walked around with huge stuffed animals they'd won; I tried but never managed to win one of the big prizes. Attending the Mid South Fair and eating cotton candy while listening to the clack-clack of the huge wooden roller coaster called the Pippin was an exciting experience for someone who had just left the country for the city.

એ

The Hotel Chisca in Memphis housed a local radio station that featured some well-known disc jockeys, including Wink Martindale and the popular but eccentric Dewey Phillips, the first man to play Elvis Presley's music on the radio. Since the hotel stood adjacent to the YWCA where we lived, some fellow students and I often visited the station to watch Wink Martindale host his radio show. Wink was always gracious and never seemed to mind the giddy teenagers swooning over him.

Wink, a handsome man who called Memphis home, went on to host numerous television game shows including *Tic-Tac-Dough*, *High Rollers*, *What's This Song?*, and *Gambit*. He is one of only two television personalities to have hosted fifteen or more game shows.

એ

In the early twentieth century, music became Memphis's claim to fame. Blues artists, such as W. C. Handy, Aretha Franklin, and Isaac Hayes, were instrumental in turning Beale Street into the landmark it is today. In 1948, Sam Phillips opened Sun Studios on Beale Street and later launched the careers of Elvis Presley, Johnny Cash, Jerry Lee Lewis, Carl Perkins, and Roy Orbison.

"Elvis Watching" became a popular pastime among many of the local college students living in Memphis at the peak of his popularity. Although we were not Elvis fanatics who tried to climb the fence around Graceland to see him, we were always excited to get a glimpse of him in downtown Memphis or traveling on the streets around Graceland.

Later, when I lived less than a mile from Graceland, it was not unusual for me to see Elvis driving one of his Cadillacs around town or down Highway 51 in suburban Whitehaven. Dressed in casual clothes, he looked different from the onstage Elvis in his flashy costumes, but he was still handsome with his slicked-down black hair and charming smile.

While living in Whitehaven, I often ran into Elvis's girlfriend and wife-to-be, Priscilla—sometimes disguised in a blonde wig; her beauty was so overwhelming it was easy to identify her despite the wig. I thought she was the most beautiful woman I had ever seen.

Since Priscilla and I shared the same obstetrician in later years, I frequently saw her in Dr. Prentiss Turman's office when she was pregnant with Lisa Marie and I was pregnant with my son, Doug. Our children were born near the same time at Baptist Memorial Hospital in Memphis.

Elvis's dad, Vernon, and his wife Dee, were often spotted in the local Walgreen's drugstore or at one of the few restaurants in the Whitehaven area. As a child, Lisa Marie (Elvis and Priscilla's daughter) sometimes accompanied Vernon and Dee who regularly lunched at the Walgreen's café. They were friendly and never seemed to mind exchanging pleasantries with the local residents.

Having an early love of Christian music, especially that of the Blackwood Brothers and Statesmen quartets, I attended their gospel concerts held at the Ellis Auditorium in Memphis. At the time Ellis Auditorium was the largest event facility in Memphis, accommodating several thousand people.

Elvis was also a big fan of gospel music. If he wasn't on tour at the time, he attended the concerts. Due to contractual obligations, he couldn't perform, but he was always brought onstage and introduced to the excited crowd. After the concerts were over, Elvis usually invited some of the singers to Graceland where he joined them singing and playing piano for hours.

On one occasion, my friend Bonita attended the concert with me, hoping she could see Elvis. Sure enough, Elvis was there. When he was introduced, Bonita jumped up with pen and paper in hand and started running down the hallways trying to find him for an autograph. As I struggled to keep pace with her, I tried to convince her that finding him would be impossible.

Passing by a glass doorway, Bonita saw what she thought was Elvis's long black Cadillac in an alley behind the auditorium. Just as we got past the doorway, Elvis and his entourage emerged. Though she didn't get her autograph, we both got the thrill of a lifetime when he flashed his famous smile and waved to us as he got into his car, surrounded by bodyguards.

After Elvis became a star, it took him many years to return to his hometown of Memphis to perform. When he finally returned for a live concert, he disproved the myth that "you can't go home again" by selling out the twelve-thousand-seat Mid-South Coliseum in only a few hours. Tickets were a hot item, and I considered myself fortunate to get tickets for me and my family to attend.

Clara – College days

The YWCA where I lived while attending college

As my college graduation neared, the local utility company in Memphis, one of the largest in the country, contacted the school about an administrative job they wanted to fill. They asked the school to provide a list of qualified candidates to be considered for the open position, and I was recommended for an interview. I was truly fortunate and excited when I got the job—not only did I consider it a prestigious position, but the pay was more than the average salary for administrative work.

I occasionally rode the Greyhound bus back to Forrest City to spend the weekend with my family. On one such weekend, after I had worked for a while in my new job and saved some money, I asked my parents to take me to the nearest car dealership to look at cars. The dealership was ten miles away in Wynne, Arkansas. While there, I found a car I liked and could afford.

After buying the car, a 1956 Chevrolet with automatic transmission, Mama asked Daddy and me, "How are we possibly getting the car home?" I had never driven a car, and neither had she. Without hesitation, Daddy told her, "Toots will drive it home."

To everyone's relief, the scary drive home went off without incident despite our meeting a funeral procession on the narrow gravel road. In the country, it was a matter of courtesy for vehicles to pull over to the side of the road while a hearse and the long line of cars following it proceeded on their way to the cemetery. After the funeral procession passed, I pulled back onto the road and slowly followed Daddy safely home.

When I returned to Memphis that weekend, I left the car at my parents' house and practiced driving it on weekends when I returned home. When I eventually took the car to

Memphis, Mama spent a sleepless night worrying about me driving the fifty miles to Memphis on a busy highway.

℃/つ

After I had spent several years as an executive secretary at the Memphis utility's electric generating plant, the Tennessee Valley Authority (TVA) assumed operation of the plant in 1965. Fortunately TVA kept the employees who wished to stay, and as a result, my salary, benefits, and vacation time increased.

TVA, a federal agency, is the nation's largest public power provider and is completely self-financing. TVA provides power to large industries and 159 power distributors that serve some 8.8 million consumers in seven southeastern states. TVA also manages the Tennessee River and its tributaries to provide multiple benefits, including flood control, navigation, water quality, and recreation.

Later, following my husband from place to place, I transferred into other positions at different locations within TVA. As I always gave my best effort, upper management began to take notice of my work. Eventually, I was honored to become one of the few females with a management role in the company.

For the last fifteen years of my career with TVA, I served as a human resources and personnel manager. After a satisfying thirty-year career, I retired from the company in 1996.

Being instrumental in placing a severely handicapped person in a clerical position with TVA was one of the more memorable events in my career. Joe, a young man who had been handicapped as the result of a serious automobile accident, badly wanted to come to work for the company. TVA was constructing the world's largest nuclear plant in the small town of Hartsville, Tennessee, just outside Nashville. Employment opportunities were scarce in the area, and jobs at the nuclear plant were highly sought after due to the good salaries and work stability. Joe completed several employment applications and was very persistent with follow-up visits. Though he was physically limited in what he could do, I found a job I thought he could perform. He eagerly accepted the position and showed up for employment processing.

Due to the large number of people who were employed on a daily basis to supplement construction crews, the company had an on-site doctor. The doctor, who performed pre-employment medical evaluations, had a colorful and controversial manner. When Joe showed up at the medical office, the belligerent doctor called my boss and asked, "Who is the clown that sent this person for a medical evaluation?" My boss, who was aware of the situation, calmed the doctor and explained the job Joe would be doing if employed. The doctor pronounced the young man fit to do the job.

After Joe was hired, I pulled him aside and let him know that I'd stuck my neck out for him and he had better not make me regret it. Imagine my pride when a year later he went on to become the Tennessee governor's Outstanding Handicapped Employee of the Year.

*Chapter 13*

♣

*Marriage*

## Author's Note

*Family members on both Chuck's side of the family and mine were deeply affected by our eventual divorce. They were, understandably, confused and hurt upon learning of our decision to terminate our marriage. It seems, now that an appropriate time has passed, they deserve to know some of the events and situations that directly contributed to the dissolution of our marriage. Inside these pages, I have finally thrown aside a lifetime's restraint against exposing my personal and private life. I hope that doing so now will result in a better understanding of what directly contributed to the collapse of our marriage.*

*I hold my ex-husband and his family in highest regard and always will. It is my hope that they will understand that my intention in writing these pages is not to hurt anyone but solely to relate many events that led to the end of our marriage and thereby demystify its conclusion.*

Shortly after the beginning of my career I started dating my future husband, Chuck Palmer. He was the college roommate of my future brother-in-law, Don, who was dating my sister Marilyn. Don introduced Chuck and me, and we began dating in September 1961 when Don and Chuck were seniors at Memphis State University.

Chuck was a quiet person when just the two of us were present, but he became more outgoing when other people were around. I thought he was one of the nicest people I had ever met. While we were dating, he was always kind and never tried to take advantage of me, unlike some of the other college guys I had dated.

Chuck and I started out double-dating with Don and Marilyn. Since Chuck and Don were college roommates, it was only natural that we would all go out together. Don and Chuck were great fun to be around, providing many happy memories for the four of us.

Don and Chuck enjoyed relating humorous incidents that had happened in their dorm and joking about dates they went on together that hadn't worked out as planned. For example, there was the time they took Chuck's date home after she had had too much to drink. Don and Chuck helped her out of the car, took her to her parents' front door, propped her against the wall, rang the doorbell—and ran.

Don, witty and with a tremendous personality, had the ability to bring out the best in people, especially Chuck. That was the Chuck I fell in love with.

Chuck, the youngest of three children, was born about thirty miles east of Memphis in Mason, Tennessee, a tiny town known for its wooden sidewalks and nightspots. Practically any Saturday night in Mason, you can find revelers partying along the tiny false storefronts and wooden sidewalks.

Chuck's family called him "the runt" while he was growing up, as he was smaller in stature than his older brother and sister. He and his older brother, Robert, were only fifteen months apart, but Robert, being much larger, took advantage of Chuck's smaller build and bullied him as a child. If Chuck told his parents what happened, Robert would be punished—and then would beat Chuck up again for telling on him.

Chuck's mother, Kate, was a tall woman, close to six feet. Robert and Sister Lucy were tall like their mother; Chuck inherited his father's height—about five feet, ten inches. Mrs. Palmer, an intelligent woman, kept books and did the accounting for their horse racing business. She was a great cook who could prepare a good meal seemingly out of nothing.

Robert, a fine, upstanding member of the Mason community today, was a popular high school football player. He spent his teenage years with the football team, practicing and playing in games after school. Chuck came home from school and attended to chores that had to be done. When I asked why he had to do all the work, Chuck always replied, "That's just the way it was."

At times Chuck talked to me about feeling as though he didn't measure up to the expectations of his family and wondering whether he was truly loved by his parents, whom he felt didn't love him as they did his older brother.

I felt Chuck had emotional scars from his growing-up years. I understood perfectly because I had had some of the same feelings as I was growing up. Though my mother was a warm and loving person, affection was never shown by either of my parents to each other or to their children. Like Chuck, I also felt my parents had favorites.

Chuck's father, unknown to many, was a functioning alcoholic. Mr. Palmer didn't drink publicly but entered rehab at times to dry out. Sometimes, he went years without taking a drink; but once he did, it became a problem. To his credit, he never allowed alcohol to interfere with his work. Despite his disease, Mr. Palmer became a very successful harness racehorse owner, driver, and trainer.

Once, shortly after we started dating, Chuck called, and I could tell he was upset. He asked if he could come over and take me to eat. When we drove to one of the local drive-in restaurants, he parked the car, drew me close, and just sat there. I kept waiting for him to tell me what was wrong, but he wouldn't say what was bothering him. I later learned that his dad had started drinking again after staying off liquor for several years. The whole family was devastated, but Chuck couldn't bring himself to talk to me about it.

Chuck and I dated only four months before he asked me to marry him in December 1961. We married the following year, on March 24, 1962, two months before his college graduation.

In the months before our wedding, and on our wedding day, I was so filled with love for Chuck that it was blatantly obvious, many said, in how my eyes sparkled and shined at the slightest glimpse of him, reflecting the deep feelings in my heart that I had never known I could experience toward any man. He was the fulfillment of every dream I'd ever wished for in a husband during the long days and years of my growing up. Chuck was considerate and loving toward me, loyal to his original family and to me as his new one, so tender, kind and compassionate. In short, he was a good man, a decent man.

Our wedding took place in the small country church I had attended while growing up in New Castle. The Palmer family had never been to New Castle or met my family prior to our marriage. They were surprised at how far out in the country my parents lived—not what they had expected. Good-natured comments directed at Chuck ("How did you find her way back in these woods?") kept us laughing, but I sensed some seriousness in their comments.

On our wedding day, Chuck's sister-in-law, Robin, who owned a beauty shop in Mason, washed her hair just before she left home for the wedding. Since it was a warm day and they had no air conditioning in their car, they drove with the windows rolled down. As their car followed Chuck and his parents over the dry gravel roads, dust rolled in through the windows and created mud in her still-damp hair. Robin, a good sport, took it in stride and enjoyed relating the story over the years.

The small country church was packed, and the wedding was nice; but my brother-in-law walked me down the aisle since Daddy refused to do so. In fact, Daddy had not planned to attend the wedding until, for the first time, I nervously challenged him to not disappoint me. To my surprise he did attend but left immediately after the wedding and didn't attend the reception. It wasn't that Daddy had anything against my marrying Chuck. He hadn't attended any of his kids' high school graduations or weddings. Daddy had friends but was anti-social when it came to attending activities with his family.

Gene and Marion Horton, some close friends in the New Castle community who had a lovely home, were kind enough to volunteer to host my wedding reception. As a teenager, I had babysat for them, and I was fond of their two small sons, John and Carl.

Their long country-style ranch house had a large glassed-in area that was the perfect place for a wedding reception. The wide, manicured front lawn with towering oak trees made the setting even more perfect.

Years later Mama told me, "At your wedding and reception, I was left with the impression Mrs. Palmer felt we were beneath her." Mama, usually a quiet person who looked for good in everyone, said she made a special effort to become acquainted with my new mother-in-law and make her feel welcome, but Mrs. Palmer didn't seem interested in having anything to do with her.

I was oblivious to any perceived slights, and my wedding day was one of the happiest days of my life. My thoughts were of Chuck as I wondered how one man could be so many wonderful things and how such a man could choose me as his wife. I vowed to myself to do everything in my power to love him and make him proud of me that March day and in the years to come of our expected forever-together lives.

During our honeymoon in Hot Springs, Arkansas, Chuck was loving and considerate. It seemed every wish of mine was exactly what he wanted too. We had a great time attending the horse races at Oaklawn Park and just enjoying the scenery. I didn't think it possible to be so happy, and I looked forward to the many days and years ahead of loving and cherishing my husband.

If I had known then that those perfect days would lead to another perfect being entering our lives, the joy for us both would have been limitless. Our first son was conceived during this time, and I would have had it no other way then or now. But, by the time of his birth, the first hairline cracks in our marriage had started making their tiny appearances and even culminated in insensitive treatment of that sacred event, known since time began as one of life's most blessed and most precious.

❧

A long ascending driveway in the countryside near Mason led to the Palmer farm. Adam and his wife, Kate, lived on the sixty-acre farm, which had been in Mrs. Palmer's family since 1796 when Tennessee was settled as a state.

Mr. Palmer, for many years a policeman and town marshal for Mason, had a love for horses but had only dealt with horses and mules on the farm. In 1953, after attending a Trade Day in Mason (similar to our modern-day flea markets), he saw a nice horse and bought him.

A friend of Mr. Palmer's was doing some harness racing, so he and the friend decided to take his newly purchased horse to a fair in Paducah, Kentucky. Mr. Palmer raced him and finished fourth. After that, he said later, he was hooked. He started looking for some better horses and learned of a man in nearby Brownsville, Tennessee, who had four

144

horses and some equipment for sale; and with that, he was in business.

He raced in county fairs in Kentucky and advanced to New Orleans. He raced numerous small tracks in Michigan, Ohio, Pennsylvania, and California. Mr. Palmer, a keen observer, listened to a lot of people and watched and learned their riding techniques to develop his own.

The Palmers spent most of their time in Chicago. After living in apartments and motels, they eventually purchased a thirty-two-foot travel trailer, which they lived in during the racing season. They came back to Mason each October for the winter months.

Mr. Palmer was selected the leading driver and trainer in Chicago in 1970. The same year, Illinois Horse of the Year honors went to Song Cycle, the pacer he trained and drove for its owner. This was the only time that both driver and horse were selected for these honors in the same year.

Kay Michael proved to be the Palmers' best horse. The horse started in Chicago and made more than three hundred thousand dollars during his lifetime. He became known from coast to coast. Kay Michael's mother and colt were also raised on the Palmer farm.

Mr. Palmer, an early riser, began his day at 6:00 A.M. when he went to the barn to work with and care for as many as twenty-one horses. As many as nine trainers and grooms would begin their tasks at Palmer Stables by opening up his big red barn and harnessing the horses in preparation for training. The huge barn, which still stands, was spacious enough for twenty horses.

The training track at the Palmer farm was delicately carved from a rolling pasture near their home. A lake was formed inside the track, and visitors could sit in the barn office and look out a picture window as the horses circled the track. Each horse ran three or four miles around the half-mile track before lunch. Every horse had a trunk containing all its proper gear, for example, blankets and harnesses. The driver's attire had to meet special specifications as well; Mr. Palmer's colors, maroon and black, were registered with the U.S. Trotters Association.

Mr. Palmer did more than train the horses, however. Not content to sit back and watch someone else reap what he had sown, he manned the surreys. Surreys were buggies ridden by drivers during the races. During twenty-two years in the business, he earned a reputation as one of the top drivers on the Chicago circuit.

Mr. Palmer and his horses accumulated an impressive track record beginning in 1953 when he first entered the harness race in Paducah for a two-hundred-dollar purse. His winnings eventually neared the $2.5 million mark with 542 first-place finishes before he retired in 1985.

In December 1992 the Illinois Harness Horsemen's Association inducted Mr. Palmer into the Illinois Harness Racing Hall of Fame. Sixteen family members, including me, gathered in Chicago on December 6. Illinois Governor John Edgar was present, along with 450 fellow harness drivers and owners.

In introducing Mr. Palmer, Governor Edgar stated that over the course of his career, which had begun in 1953 and continued until his retirement in 1985, Mr. Palmer had driven in approximately three thousand races, winning 615 of them. He was compared to race car driver Richard Petty, but my father-in-law had won three times as many races.

❧

My very first experience with disillusionment in our marriage came a few months after Chuck and I married. Don graduated from college and chose to enter the air force in lieu of being drafted into the army. After Don left, Chuck never seemed to be the same person. He became quiet and withdrawn—a different person without Don around.

It was evident from the start of our marriage that Chuck and I had problems with communication. After our marriage, this was intensified by my own feelings of inadequacy. Having had a father who ruled the household with an iron fist, I was reluctant to express my feelings for fear I would do or say something to cause friction between us. Also, growing up in the country, I had led a sheltered life; I was socially immature and naive. Chuck and I had both grown up in dysfunctional families and lacked the maturity to deal with our conflicting emotions.

I believe Chuck meant well, but it became obvious that, since he didn't have an example of normal family life, he was a victim of circumstances. His family was unemotional and stoic. While his parents loved their children, they had created a cold atmosphere in the Palmer household.

While we did have some good times while visiting Chuck's parents, the experience was sometimes painful. Occasionally someone spoke, but we mostly sat and looked out the window. Many years later, after our sons were grown, they joked about the "one time we saw our grandfather smile."

In later years, our son Scott commented that the reason his dad was distant and unemotional was because that was the way his family had been when he was growing up—that was all he knew.

❦

A few months after Chuck and I married, as we sat around the dinner table at his parents' house, his mother told the story of a friend whose son had recently married.

After the son's wedding, he found that his wife needed a great amount of dental work and he would be responsible for the bills. After telling the story, Mrs. Palmer looked toward me and asked, "And how are *your* teeth?" I managed to say in a timid voice that my teeth were fine.

I felt she was alluding to the fact that since I grew up poor, I probably had never received proper dental care. Actually, my teeth were in great condition since, during college, I had kept dental appointments every Saturday for a year at the Tennessee College of Dentistry in Memphis. Since the students were residents-in-training, the dental work was free. It wasn't unusual to make several trips to have one tooth filled, but they did excellent work.

&

Two months after our wedding, a visit to the doctor confirmed I was pregnant, which meant I had conceived during the first month of our marriage. Our first child was due to be born on December 24, 1962—exactly nine months from our wedding day.

Though the pregnancy was unplanned and came soon after the beginning of our marriage, I was excited to be expecting a baby. Chuck, however, seemed to withdraw into a chilling silence. Years later, he told me his attitude during my pregnancy and the difficult months after our son's birth was the result of fear. "I knew nothing about babies," he said.

As a senior in college, Chuck was interested in attending Air Force Candidate School and becoming a pilot. Upon graduation, he successfully passed the required tests but, due to poor eyesight, was disqualified from pilot training. He instead chose to enter the air force as a second lieutenant and become a navigator. This was shortly after the beginning of the Vietnam War, and the draft was in effect.

After I became pregnant, Chuck had the option of getting a deferment or continuing with his plans to join the air force. He struggled with the decision but decided to take the deferment. He graduated from college in May that year but had mixed feelings about his decision not to enter the military.

As my pregnancy progressed, Chuck's feelings of guilt over his decision to forfeit his military career were magnified by the coolness I felt from him. His mother was vocal in her opinion that he should have gone into the air force as planned.

*Chapter 14*

♣

*Children*

Our first son, Scott, was born in 1962. During the ninth month of my pregnancy, when Dr. Turman examined me on one of my weekly visits, he said I could go into labor at any time. If that didn't happen during the night, however, he told me, I should be at the hospital early the next morning and he would induce labor. I have often wondered if Scott was ready to be born, or if Dr. Turman just wanted to get me in and out of the hospital before Christmas. At that time, it was customary to spend three or four days in the hospital after the baby's birth.

Scott was born at 12:20 P.M. on a cold December day. Chuck took me to the hospital but wasn't there during labor and childbirth. He said he didn't like hospitals and left to have lunch with a friend. After Scott was born, the doctor was unable to find a family member to tell we had a beautiful baby boy.

At the time, doctors used "twilight sleep" during labor and delivery. Twilight sleep is a type of sedation that is administered intravenously to make the patient sleepy and calm during a labor. The patient is typically awake, but groggy, and able to follow instructions.

After Scott was born, I heard nurses in the recovery room discussing the absence of my husband and other family members. I remember hearing one of them say as I began awakening, "Did Dr. Turman ever find anybody to tell about this baby being born?" Although Chuck had returned to the hospital by that time, I knew I had been alone during the birth.

Chuck's family came to visit and see the new baby at the hospital that night. Everyone was friendly, and Chuck's parents seemed happy about the birth of their fourth grandchild. What happened over the next few days was never explained to me, but while I was still in the hospital, events took a tumultuous turn.

Before Scott was born, Chuck decided his mother would stay with me for two or three days after I returned home from the hospital. This wasn't discussed with me; I preferred to have my own mother with me but didn't want to upset their plans and cause a problem.

When it came time for me to leave the hospital, I was told I would be going for a week to my in-laws' house instead of mine. When I asked why, Chuck said, "Oh, well, Mama got upset, so we're just going out there." He didn't say why she was upset, and I didn't ask. When we got to her house, I discovered she had taken her Christmas tree down and thrown it in the backyard although it was still three days before Christmas.

On Christmas Day, there was no evidence at the Palmer house of it being Christmas—in fact it was never mentioned. Mrs. Palmer was a great cook, but on Christmas Day we had a sparse meal consisting of fried pork chops, pinto beans, and slaw—no ham, turkey, pie, cake, or anything related to a traditional Christmas dinner.

I soon began to feel my mother-in-law resented our being at her house. Chuck was working in Memphis, about thirty miles away, and left the afternoon of Christmas Day to return to our home. I desperately wanted to go home with him, but again, I wouldn't speak up.

I had known my in-laws for only six months before Chuck and I married, and during that time had been around them very little. We were practically strangers. To be left alone at such a sensitive time as the birth of our first child was unfair to both my in-laws and me.

As the week progressed, I became deeply depressed. I couldn't eat because of a lump in my throat and a hollow feeling in the pit of my stomach. Already thin when I became pregnant, I had gained only fifteen pounds during pregnancy. Scott weighed almost eight pounds at birth, and the delivery had taken its toll on me. According to Dr. Turman, I had an unusual amount of stitches, and sitting was agonizing.

Scott was a colicky baby from the beginning, awake and crying most of the night after leaving the hospital. I was up with him alone every night during that week with little or no sleep. Other than Mrs. Palmer bathing him each morning, I had no help.

Once in the middle of the night, weakness overcame me, and I fell to the floor with Scott in my arms. Fortunately, he wasn't hurt, so I cradled and cried with him while lying on the floor. Nearing a breaking point, I desperately needed and wanted my husband.

The logical solution would have been for Chuck to come and get me. I kept hoping he would call to see how we were doing, but he never did. He had been gone since the previous Sunday, so finally on Thursday I made a long-distance call and asked him to bring some clothes for me when he came the next afternoon after work. My feet were swollen, and I couldn't wear shoes, so I asked him to bring the diuretic medication I had taken for my swollen feet during pregnancy.

He said he would bring the items but didn't ask how either the baby or I was doing. It was more like a business call that lasted less than a minute. I could have done without the items, but I really wanted to talk to *him*. I felt more depressed than ever after making the call.

Knowing how conservative Mrs. Palmer was, I felt I should pay for the long-distance call to Chuck. After the call, I asked the operator to call back with time and charges; the cost amounted to ninety-three cents.

When I gave my mother-in-law a dollar bill for the

phone call, she berated me for not reversing the charges to our phone. In my depressed state, it was almost more than I could bear when she shook the dollar bill at me and said, "This money will be gone by the time the bill comes in, and I will end up having to pay for your phone call."

The highlight of that week came when my sister-in-law Robin, who operated a small beauty shop in the back of the Palmers' house, insisted on shampooing and setting my hair. Refusing to take pay, Robin kindly said that it was the least she could do.

Friday finally came as I eagerly awaited Chuck's arrival that afternoon to take us home the next day. After getting to the house and eating an early dinner, Chuck announced he was going to bed because he had been working late that week and was tired. Desperately wanting attention from him and needing emotional support, I lay in bed beside him as soon as Scott went to sleep. As soon as I lay down, Scott woke up crying. I was up with him, alone, most of that night.

While it was good to get home the next day, the next few months were trying for both of us. Chuck helped with Scott's care, but Scott's colic kept both of us up most nights until we were exhausted. Various recommendations from our pediatrician did little to help.

It was during this time that I began to ponder disturbing thoughts concerning my relationship with Chuck, but I excused them away. Though I didn't know the name for it, I was in a deep postpartum depression, and the lack of emotional support from my husband contributed to the problem. In later years he attributed his actions to being scared of the responsibility of a wife and baby.

I returned to full-time work when Scott was two months old. I was fortunate to find a lady to take care of him during the day and help with the housework.

We had bought a small house shortly before Scott was born. The house was nice but didn't have modern appliances like a dishwasher or clothes dryer. The routine of coming home from work and then taking care of the baby and preparing dinner was exhausting. It would have been nice to have help cleaning up after dinner and washing dishes, but Chuck had made it clear from the start of our marriage that his father had never washed dishes and neither would he.

Scott's colic eventually got better, and Chuck and I were able to get some sleep; however, there was a distance in our marriage. It was as if I was always trying to prove to myself and to him that I was good enough for him. In a way he was good to me, but his lack of emotion and affection took its toll.

Around his family, Chuck rarely acknowledged me. Not usually included in family conversations, I sometimes felt like an outsider. Over the years, when insulting or unkind comments were made to me in Chuck's presence, he never once spoke up or said anything in my defense. I believe if he had supported me or spoken up on my behalf, things would have been different between us.

Chuck's sister, Lucy, lived not far from us. A kind person, Lucy was gracious to us over the years. Since she was the oldest of the three children, she had at times been responsible for her two younger siblings, especially Chuck. Chuck was very close to Lucy.

The lack of communication between Chuck and me was intensified by his long nightly telephone conversations with Lucy. I usually found out what was going on in his life from his side of these conversations. She called after dinner, and they talked for over an hour nearly every night for many years, leaving me feeling shut out of his life. Lucy was an intelligent lady, and Chuck inevitably took her side and opinions over anything I had to say.

I wouldn't allow myself to admit to anyone—not even my family—how I was struggling. I kept my emotions inside, letting no one know how I was hurting. I pushed aside and denied disturbing thoughts that tried to surface as I began to wonder if my marriage was a mistake. My own negative thoughts kept me down, with the depression and resentment continuing for several years.

At three years old, Scott began making a terrible wheezing sound when he breathed. When he became active, his lips and fingertips turned blue. After several trips to the doctor proved unsuccessful, the pediatrician had him hospitalized for a lung exploration. I was terrified, as the doctors told us it would be necessary to stop his breathing during the exploration, which involved running a tube with a camera into his lung.

On the day of Scott's surgery, as I pulled my crying son's arms from around my neck and handed him to a nurse, I watched with tears and a heavy heart as he disappeared down a long corridor where the glass doors read, "Stop. Surgical staff only."

When I returned to the hospital room to wait with Chuck while Scott was in surgery, the staff brought in a complimentary plate of food. I gave it to Chuck since I was too nervous to eat. "I don't want it. I'm going out to find a restaurant and eat lunch," he said, leaving me alone and terrified during our son's surgery.

By the time Chuck returned, Scott was in the recovery room, and the doctor had brought by a piece of raw potato that had lodged in his lung and set up an infection. The infection had caused the lung to become swollen, preventing air from getting through. After the surgery and a day in an oxygen tent, Scott was released from the hospital.

By the time Scott was four years old I began thinking of having another child; I didn't want him to grow up an only child. At first Chuck was reluctant, but he eventually came around. He changed jobs about that time and had to go away for four weeks' training. While he was gone, I discovered I was pregnant, but I waited until he got home to tell him the news.

Nine months later, our son Douglas was born. According to Chuck's brother-in-law, James, he and Chuck ate lunch together at a local restaurant as I was giving birth.

Douglas was a good baby. He didn't have the severe colic that Scott had, and we were able to get more sleep. The recovery period was also quite different that time, as my mother came to stay with me. She was a lifesaver, and I didn't fall into the deep depression I had suffered the first time.

**Scott, Douglas, and Clara**

*Chapter 15*

❧

*Nashville*

I returned to work part-time for a couple of years after Douglas was born and then returned to full-time work with TVA. Chuck was good at his work, so after a few years at his job, he was promoted to a new position. Since the job was with the Tennessee State government, we moved to Nashville in 1974, down the road from the Grand Ole Opry.

I was fortunate to be able to transfer to Nashville with TVA and continue my career. Persevering through inevitable obstacles and challenges while in the Nashville area, I began moving upward within the company and eventually into management.

Chuck worked for the State government for several years as chief of compliance in Tennessee's OSHA program. While with the State, he received an offer from TVA to accept a management position in their health and safety program. He accepted the offer, but unfortunately, the job was in Alabama. After starting the job, he commuted on weekends from Nashville to Alabama for several years.

When Chuck accepted the job in Alabama, we had just built a new home in Gallatin, Tennessee, a small town outside of Nashville. Scott was a bright and serious student in his junior year of high school, and we didn't feel it was in his best interest to move him at the time. My career was going well, and neither of us was anxious to move. I felt sorry for Chuck having to miss so much home life and his sons' growing-up years. I knew he missed it, but we both felt we were doing the right thing.

In addition to commuting home each weekend, Chuck's job required other travel. The TVA agency where we worked covered a seven-state region. Chuck said that, as he traveled throughout the valley and visited different offices, he was amazed at the number of people who knew of me and the position I held in the company. He was particularly impressed when in senior-management meetings he frequently met people who, according to him, were very complimentary of me. He said he'd had no idea of the reputation I held within the company. He would repeat what others said but never express his own feelings.

Having never had much attention from my husband, I looked to my job as a source of fulfillment. Even though I worked hard and had stressful jobs during much of my career, I felt the self-esteem acquired over the years had made me a totally different person from the one I had been—not only the timid, insecure person I had been when working in the fields and attending elementary and high school, but also the person I was when Chuck and I first married.

In thirty-seven years of married life, I can never remember receiving a compliment from my husband. Friends often complimented Chuck on his wife and told him he was fortunate to have someone like me. His response was always the same, "Well, I don't give her compliments, but if I see something I don't like, I'll let her know." He seemed to enjoy repeating, "I don't tell her nice things about herself because I don't want her to get a big head." I don't think he realized how such crushing comments made me feel, but I felt he expected me to be the perfect wife regardless of how demoralized I was.

Once, my mother-in-law surprised me by saying, in Chuck's presence, how nice she thought I looked that day. Afterward she looked at Chuck, I suppose waiting for him to say something. When he didn't comment, she told him, "You better start telling her how pretty she is, or someone else will." I was so surprised my mouth flew open, but Chuck remained silent.

Commuting was hard for Chuck, and me as well, with me having full responsibility of running the household and working full-time while he was away. It was extremely hard handling on my own everything that came up during the week as Chuck was miles away until the weekend. By then Scott was away at college. Thankfully, Douglas was a responsible teenager who seemed to realize he was the man of the house while his dad was gone. Having an innate sense of responsibility, he helped with chores around the house and was not only good company but a comfort to me as well.

During one particularly stressful period in Nashville, my job required extensive travel, sometimes daily. I got out of bed at 3:00 A.M., left home at 4:00 A.M., and traveled ninety miles to the TVA office in Drakesboro, Kentucky, to get there by 7:00 A.M. I usually had a room full of construction workers to hire by the time I got there. After a stressful day, I returned home by six or seven at night and did the same thing the next day.

Surprisingly, on a weekend visit to my parents' home, Daddy expressed his displeasure with me having such a stressful job. "You should quit that damn job," he said. "You have no business traveling that much and working those long hours." I felt like a child being chastised and couldn't help but think how ironic it was: Daddy being concerned about me working too hard!

From all outside appearances, Chuck and I had a good marriage. We shared an interest in sports and enjoyed attending sporting events together over the years. We enjoyed reading the newspaper together and discussing current events. We could talk about the world situation— but never about ourselves, our emotions, or our problems. I was careful never to reveal a problem outside our marriage so as to protect our vows to honor, love, and cherish each other.

We always had a nice home that was well maintained

inside and out. Chuck took pride in our lawn and did a good job taking care of it. He was a good father to our two sons, although I felt he was sometimes too quick to administer harsh discipline.

Despite our problems, there *were* good times when the boys were growing up. Every summer Chuck, the boys, and I looked forward to a family vacation. Early vacations were spent camping on the shores of Lake Norfork near Mountain Home, Arkansas. I enjoyed the beautiful scenery and crystal clear waters. Camping with Maxine and her husband, Gene, we always managed to have at least one big fish fry with fish caught by the guys.

We later bought a small travel trailer for camping vacations at Lake Norfork, but since most of our trips were spent in areas around the lake with no electricity, the hundred-degree heat was unbearable in the small trailer without air conditioning.

While I appreciated the beauty of the area, most of my time was spent fighting the heat while taking care of Scott and Douglas as the other adults fished, swam, and water-skied. Knowing how much Chuck enjoyed the trips and feeling it was important to get the boys out of the city to experience nature, I did my best to ignore the inconveniences.

Some of my favorite vacation memories are of family trips that Chuck, the boys, and I took with my sisters and their families to Fort Walton Beach and Destin, Florida. These vacation spots were the perfect place to relax. We lounged and walked along the white sandy beaches on the Gulf of Mexico, and the water was shallow enough for us to feel comfortable letting the kids swim and play on the beach. Renting a motel room and eating fresh seafood made for the ideal vacation.

When Scott and Douglas became teenagers, we spent most summer vacations at Fairfield Bay, a lovely resort area in the Ozark Mountains of Arkansas. All my siblings, their spouses, and their children would occupy a large condo for a week.

John and Glenda, who lived in the area, generously shared their speedboat and pontoon boat with the rest of the family. Taking the pontoon boat out to a secluded cove on Greers Ferry Lake, we enjoyed the rock cliffs, clear blue water, and beautiful scenery of the Ozarks. After packing a picnic lunch, we would spend each day swimming and water-skiing—and in my case, floating on a life raft safely secured in a life jacket!

Sunset was the best time of day. Watching the sky turn from blue to pink and orange as the sun slowly lowered and disappeared over the water was a fitting end to many perfect days.

# Chapter 16

♣

## *Alabama*

By 1984 I felt the job in Nashville was adversely affecting my health. The long hours and extensive travel demanded everything I had. I lived at a pace at which few can survive for long. I was burning out. I discussed resigning with Chuck, but he told me then as he had before, "If you quit your job, I'll quit mine."

Knowing I couldn't keep up my frenetic pace indefinitely, I requested a transfer to TVA's Browns Ferry Nuclear Plant, which was located in Alabama near Chuck's job. The only position available with TVA at the Alabama location was an administrative position that required a 50 percent salary cut. Despite management promotions and a good salary at the Nashville location, I accepted the position in Alabama. As a result of my transfer, TVA paid to sell our house and took care of moving expenses.

After moving to Alabama, Chuck and I lived in an apartment for nine months while building a home in a beautiful area between Florence and Decatur called Turtle Point Village. I loved the house and the area, although it was thirty-five miles from my office.

After working for three months at the nuclear plant, I was summoned to the president's office, having no idea why I was being asked to meet with him. He explained that his executive assistant was leaving, and he went on to express an interest in having me apply for the job. Since it was a promotion, I applied and, when I was hired, was able to recoup some of the salary cut I had taken.

Six months after I began working as the president's assistant, I was again summoned to his office along with the director of personnel. "Clara," said the president, "the reason I brought you into my office to work as my assistant was for you to learn the organization. Now we want to offer you a management position as human resource officer in the personnel director's office." I was thrilled, as my salary was reinstated to what it had been before the transfer.

Although my job was stressful and involved working long hours, I was proud to be the first female manager among three thousand employees at the nuclear plant in Alabama. Having to be at the office by 7:00 A.M. required getting up at 4:30 A.M. After making the seventy-mile round trip to the office, I usually came home exhausted and prepared dinner for the family each night.

After several years of feeling unappreciated and keeping everything inside, I made the mistake of telling Chuck that I didn't feel I loved him. I could tell he was deeply hurt and worried that he would lose me. He said, "Well, I know how to fix that." He started sending flowers to my office a couple of times a week, but nothing else changed. I enjoyed the flowers and kept them on my desk. At first I told him how much I appreciated the flowers, but after several weeks, it got old.

One day as I walked in the house after a long day's work, Chuck asked if I had gotten his flowers. I made another mistake, saying, "I don't need more flowers—I need help with my workload and some rest." I never received flowers from him again, and he never let me forget my remark; but I understood his frustration.

My friend Debbie, who was married to a policeman, had related to me that she prided herself in always providing for her husband's needs. For years, I kept that in mind and tried my best to do the same even though my heart wasn't always in it. Later in our marriage, I faced the reality that I was just going through the motions. I respected Chuck, but he became more like a big brother than a husband. The lack of interest on my part left me feeling guilty and frustrated by my inability to have a satisfying relationship with him.

I have been asked why, since I was economically

independent, I stayed in the marriage for so long. I never considered a divorce as long as my children were home, although at times, our relationship was more like a business arrangement than a marriage.

Any time friends or relatives said something about men finding me attractive, Chuck responded "I don't have to worry about that. She can't take care of what she has at home." On the contrary, many opportunities presented themselves through the years. Some I knew about, but others I didn't recognize until after the fact.

In one of my first jobs as an executive secretary, being naive, I had no idea my boss had feelings for me until I left and found out through my replacement. In frustration she called one day to ask for help on a project. She said that, regardless of how well she did her job, her boss was never satisfied because he still had "stars in his eyes" for me. I was shocked and told her I knew he thought well of me but had no idea he felt that way.

There were others along the way, but I kept my distance since I was married and had no interest in any of them—until John came along.

The day he walked into my office and our eyes met, I felt a chemistry I had never experienced with anyone before. Our friendship developed quite unexpectedly, and we were amazed at how we came to be such important parts of each other's lives.

As our friendship deepened, feelings that had long been dormant in me began to surface. John was in a high-level position with the company, and with my being in management also, any involvement along romantic lines was a strict no-no within the company. That didn't prevent us from talking to each other when we had a chance at the office or going out for occasional lunches.

Chuck has blamed the eventual failure of our marriage, to a great extent, on my experiences as a child and the fact that I wouldn't let go of my past. When we began having serious trouble in our marriage, he often referred to the barriers and walls I had built between us. My feeling was that he was largely responsible for the walls being there and I couldn't climb over them; his years of insensitivity had constructed those walls brick by brick.

I felt I was expected to be the perfect career woman with a well-paying job, along with being a mother, a housekeeper, and the perfect wife—all with no expression of the approval, appreciation, or affection that I badly needed. Looking back, I must admit I had a deep-seated need for approval and a desire to please those around me, which, in all likelihood, can be traced back to my early childhood.

Other than not speaking up when things bothered me, most of the mistakes I made in our marriage were not my parents' fault. For all my dad's shortcomings, he taught us the value of work; that is where I inherited my work ethic, and it has served me well. He also taught us that anything worth doing was worth doing right. My childhood made me a more determined person, and I view that as a positive. Looking back on the bad things, I now realize they were what prepared me for life.

❧

After our two sons completed college and were out on their own pursuing successful careers, it was all the more obvious that my life had revolved around them. Their college graduations were the two proudest days of my life. Chuck and I were elated with what they had done with their lives.

Scott is an achiever—a bright man with an honors degree in engineering. Doug, who is in the medical field, is a commonsense person whose good humor lights up a room when he enters. He is also an accomplished musician and golfer. I call them my stars and sunshine, and my love for and faith in them has never faltered. One thing Chuck and I both agree on is that "we did *something* right" while bringing them up.

As TVA was downsizing in the early 1990s, Chuck lost his job and accepted a position with a company back in Memphis, which we still considered home. Again, since I was working in Alabama with TVA, he lived and worked in Memphis and commuted to our Alabama home on weekends.

Eventually, the strain of living apart caught up with Chuck and me. It was like we were not connected and becoming out of touch. We didn't admit it to ourselves or each other, but it was clear both of us were lonely.

Since we both had family in the Memphis area, I sometimes traveled to Memphis on weekends rather than having him come to Alabama. This continued for several years until I was able to transfer to Memphis with TVA. We bought a nice home, and the two of us settled in, hoping for a new beginning as the start of our golden years was nearing.

I had heard of empty nest syndrome but had not paid much attention until it applied to Chuck and me. Since we had basically lived apart for thirteen of our last twenty years of marriage, it was a tremendous adjustment not only to live together full-time again but also to have just the two of us at home.

We both felt a distance between us, but staying true to my commitment, I did my best to be cooperative. However, I was continually left with the impression that intimacy was the most important part of our marriage as far as Chuck was concerned—that everything else was irrelevant. I knew it was important but didn't feel it should define the entire relationship, especially after thirty-five years of marriage. From my observation of marriage, I felt that passion and romance come and go through the seasons of life but that what carries couples through the hard times are shared values and common goals.

Always a private person, I felt keeping a strong outward appearance before others after any detrimental actions by my husband or any close member of the family was, justified or not, a demonstration of my loyalty to them and my respect for our relationships. And to Chuck, my husband, I made every effort to be loyal and to honor him. Never expressing my disillusionment to anyone in his family or to my own, I stifled the hurts and kept them inside.

One such event occurred when Daddy died in June 1996 of a stomach aneurysm. Daddy was eighty-four years old and still quite active. Even though he was hard on us, I loved him. The funeral was held in Forrest City at Stevens Funeral Home. Afterward, the entire family drove out to the Adkins Home Place, where our parents had lived for fifty years.

After getting back to Memphis late that day, we ate dinner and went to bed. I couldn't believe it when Chuck became amorous. "I am emotionally and physically exhausted from Daddy's funeral," I told him. His response was, "Well, I liked the man too, but everything don't have to stop." I was hurt—even angry—and I cried silently for both my father's death and Chuck's lack of sensitivity.

As it became harder to present a strong face to family and others, I suggested a trial separation. Though Chuck was hurt and didn't feel comfortable with this, he didn't try to stop me from moving temporarily into an apartment. We remained friends during the separation and talked regularly. During this time, Chuck finally revealed to me his mother's feeling that he had married beneath the family. This came as no surprise, and I felt it explained some of the treatment I had received over the years.

After we had been separated for about nine months, I stopped by Chuck's house to pick up some mail, but when I was ready to leave, something happened and all the pent-up feelings came out. After a long talk, we both realized we still had feelings for each other and decided to reunite. I was excited to move back into the house with him, and we were happy to be together again.

Shortly after our reconciliation, Chuck and I took a wonderful trip to the Western Caribbean on a weeklong cruise. Our itinerary included great destinations: the Cayman Islands, Ochoa Rio, Jamaica, and Cozumel, Mexico. The beautifully displayed food, matching that of the finest restaurants and feeding a thousand guests simultaneously, amazed us. I especially enjoyed the times Chuck and I spent taking shore excursions and watching the ocean waves from the balcony outside our cabin at night.

During our separation, Chuck had met a woman in Arkansas and began dating her shortly before our reconciliation. She was a close friend of Glenda's ex-husband, John, and his wife (whom I'll call Janet), who lived near her. When Chuck called to tell his girlfriend that he and I were getting back together, she was devastated. John and Janet, whom we had been close to, sided with the girlfriend and wanted nothing to do with us because "Chuck hurt their friend."

This hurt. We felt if our friends had our best interests at heart, they would have been happy for us trying to save our marriage. Chuck dearly loved John, and he is as close to him as he is his own brother.

*Chapter 17*

♣

*Divorce*

Chuck and I remained together three years after reconciling. At first we were happy, but the loss of his best friend's friendship took its toll. After a couple of years we were back in the same situation we had been in before the trial separation. Chuck wasn't happy, nor was I. In my heart, I felt he deserved more than I could give him or ever would be able to give him.

Chuck began asking what I was going to do. He would say, "If you're not going to do something"—he meant move out—"then I will." I felt he wanted *me* to leave rather than him for appearance's sake.

I moved into an apartment in March 1999. We had an expensive home, and I didn't feel I could afford the payments and upkeep alone. One night after we had been separated for some time, Chuck called and asked if he could come over. "Sure," I said. When he arrived, he said "Let me ask you something … Would you consider coming back to me?" I was surprised, and after thinking it over, said, "I don't feel anything would be resolved by doing so at this point. Let's wait a while and see what happens."

Chuck filed for divorce shortly after that conversation. Clearly, I didn't give divorce procedures proper thought, or I would never have made the mistake of not obtaining an attorney during the divorce proceedings. I always thought Chuck was one of the most trustworthy people I had ever known, and I saw no reason to hire an attorney.

Once, when I had to go by Chuck's attorney's office to sign papers, the attorney told me to look him in the eye. As I did, he spoke very slowly and deliberately: "You know you can get an attorney, and there is nothing wrong with that." Looking back, I feel he was trying to tell me something since he knew what a small amount of financial resources I had agreed to and that I wasn't asking for alimony.

Chuck's attorney remarked at one point during the divorce proceedings, "This is one of the friendliest divorces I have ever seen." According to Chuck, his attorney asked him several times in reference to our financial settlement, "Is this all she's getting?"

I was agreeable to the financial settlement Chuck proposed because I didn't want to take advantage of him and, most of all, because I badly wanted to remain friends after the divorce because of our sons.

As I have mentioned previously, Chuck and I didn't fight; we rarely argued at all. Despite our other differences, we were actually friends throughout our marriage. Consequently, when we divorced, we made a promise to each other that we would remain friends, if for no other reason than for our sons and grandchildren.

Our divorce became final on October 19, 1999. We were both sixty years old and had been married thirty-seven years. On the day the papers were signed and the divorce became final, I was told Chuck and his ex-girlfriend left on an out-of-town trip.

I will always have a place in my heart for Chuck, but problems in our marriage created a wall between us that eventually became insurmountable. We both received individual and joint counseling in the latter years of our marriage, and during counseling sessions, when I spoke of my marriage, I usually started by telling the counselors that my husband "was a good man." After I talked with the counselors at length, they invariably said, "Why do you insist he is a good man when you have lived like this for so many years? He probably doesn't recognize his demeaning attitude has undermined every aspect of your relationship."

After the divorce was final, Chuck sold our house, and we divided the equity in accordance with the divorce decree. He then moved to Newport, Arkansas to be near his girlfriend. His friend, John, and his wife, who had shunned us, welcomed him back with open arms as soon as our divorce was final. They also lived in Newport, and Chuck was elated to be living near them.

Misconceptions are almost always prevalent in a divorce, especially with friends and family members. Blame is usually placed on one spouse or the other without anyone but the two people involved knowing the truth. A member of Chuck's family commented to me after the divorce, "You have to take care of a man's hormones." Comments were also made regarding the walls and barriers *I* had built up. As Chuck always told me, "You can't control what other people say or do, so ignore it."

Although our divorce was painful for our two sons, who were grown and living on their own, they complimented us on the smooth adjustment and the mature way we handled the situation, unlike so many others they were familiar with who were not as amicable.

However, one cold November night shortly after our divorce became final, I was driving home from work and had car trouble. Before the engine stopped, I managed to coast into a restaurant parking lot about five minutes from Chuck's house. Darkness had fallen, and I was alone in an area of Memphis that could be considered dangerous for someone in my situation. As I attempted to restart my car, the headlights went out, and I was in total darkness.

Doug was living in South Carolina at the time, and Scott lived twenty-five miles away in suburban Collierville, Tennessee; I realized how alone I was. About that time, I noticed an older-model car driving slowly down the street with four male occupants suspiciously looking my way. As I saw the car stop and turn around, I grabbed my cell phone and called Chuck. When the occupants in the car saw me on the phone, they drove off.

After I told Chuck my predicament with the car, he said he would run over and see if he could help. After he arrived and determined I had a dead battery, he took me to a nearby AutoZone store to get a new one. The new battery worked fine, and I thanked him and offered to pay for his trouble. He wouldn't take any money and said he was glad to help. That was the Chuck I knew.

A few days later, I received an irate phone call from Chuck. "Why did you call me for help with your car? Why didn't you call Scott?" he demanded in a condescending tone. I was speechless for a moment, as he had appeared very willing to help at the time without any indication that I had done anything wrong. I said, "Scott lives twenty-five miles away, and since you were less than five minutes from where my car broke down, I didn't think you would mind." At that point he said, "Well, next time call somebody else."

As I was thinking, "*Who is this man?*" I realized he must have been trying to impress someone. Later Chuck's mother said to me, "You know, his girlfriend gave him an ultimatum. He is to have no contact with you whatsoever."

Doug was married in January following our divorce in October. The reception was held at the plush Summit Club located on the penthouse floor of Clark Towers in Memphis. Many guests were surprised that Chuck brought his girlfriend to his son's wedding reception so soon after our divorce. His sister, Lucy, later told me, "My heart broke for you."

I hadn't seen or spoken to Chuck in over two years when another unsettling incident occurred. Our youngest son, Doug, was struggling with some personal issues, and I was concerned about him. Chuck had been in town the previous week and had spent the night with Doug. Since sons usually don't discuss personal matters with their mothers—at least mine don't—I decided to call Chuck to ask how he thought Doug was doing.

When Chuck answered, I said, "Hi, are you busy?" He answered, "No, I'm not busy." "I'm calling about Douglas," I said. "I'm wondering how you think he's doing since you recently visited him. I've been concerned about him." Minutes after I began the conversation, he interrupted me in a vicious tone of voice because I had called. I knew it was time to end the conversation and hung up. I was devastated and still couldn't control my emotions by the next morning when I went to work. Finally, some of my co-workers insisted I call one of my sons. I called Doug, and he was kind enough to come to the office and take me to lunch.

There are three things in life that, once lost, are hard to rebuild: respect, trust, and friendship. The events I have related brought an end to my friendship with Chuck and led me to lose respect and trust for someone who had shared my life and our two sons and who had promised he would be a faithful friend.

It has been said, "Broken hearts give us strength, understanding, and compassion; a heart never broken will never know the joy of being imperfect." My heart was broken. I somehow felt guilty—that I had failed and disappointed those closest to me—first and foremost, my sons, and my husband as well.

Resisting the urge to rant or get back at Chuck, I chose not to respond. As a result, I became very depressed and decided to reach out for help. After becoming familiar with my history, my doctor said he thought my depression had actually been existent since the severe postpartum depression I had experienced when Scott was born. He was able to successfully treat me, and I began to feel better than I had in years. I felt I was ready to accept myself for what I was and welcome the love of those around me.

Before her death, Mrs. Palmer and I became closer. I sometimes visited her while she was still living in her home. We had long conversations, and she gave me trinkets and some costume jewelry, which I have kept. Not surprisingly, I found that some of the impressions my former mother-in-law had of my divorce from Chuck were not as I remembered them.

When Mrs. Palmer was getting on in years and doctors determined she should not live alone, her grown children found it difficult to find someone to stay with her. Though her mind was as sharp as ever, Mrs. Palmer was concerned about the amount of toilet paper the lady hired to stay with her used each day. One morning Mrs. Palmer met the lady at the door when she came to work and handed her a small amount of toilet paper. The woman quit the job after Mrs. Palmer told her she had been using too much toilet paper and that the small amount she had just been handed was all she could have that day. She had taken all the other toilet paper out of the bathrooms.

I also visited Mrs. Palmer when she moved to an assisted living facility and sometimes took our grandson and twin granddaughters to see her. She was proud of all her grandchildren but was especially proud of her twin great granddaughters. She enjoyed the visits and usually had a bag of jellybeans to share with the three children.

On my last visit to Mrs. Palmer before her death, as I started to leave the assisted living facility, she hugged me tightly and with tears in her eyes, said, "I'm so glad you came to see me. Everything's going to be all right." And it was.

# Chapter 18

♣

## Mama and Daddy

*There are three things in life that, once gone, never come back: time, words, and opportunity.*

In 1965, Daddy, a lifelong smoker, showed his grit when he had a lung removed as part of his treatment for lung cancer. Doctors had given him a slim chance of surviving the massive surgery and even less chance of being cured. After making it through surgery and refusing to discuss radiation or chemotherapy treatments with the doctors, he went home and lived another thirty years. To my knowledge, he never smoked another cigarette.

At eighty-two years of age, as Daddy mowed the lawn on his riding mower, he mowed too close to the edge of a huge hole created by an old cistern. The wheel of the mower caught the edge of the hole toppling him and the mower to the bottom. The hole was about ten feet deep and five feet across, and he couldn't possibly climb out. After Mama discovered him, she summoned neighbors to get him out. He survived the ordeal with only a few cuts and scratches.

As our children were growing up, our family celebrated holidays by getting together with Mama and Daddy. Siblings, spouses, children, and grandchildren would pack my parents' house in New Castle, known as the Adkins Home Place. My sisters and I always brought dishes of food to lessen Mama's workload. There was a lot of laughing, joking, and good-natured teasing. The cousins were close and had fun visiting with each other.

At mealtime, adults ate at the dining room table. The kids prepared their plates and ate in the living room, sitting on the couch, floor, or wherever they could find a spot. Scott and Doug still laugh about not ever making it to the "big table" as they called the dining room table where the adults ate.

Christmas, Thanksgiving, Easter, Mother's Day, Father's Day, and our parents' birthdays were occasions to get together. Depending on where we were living at the time—Memphis, Nashville, or Alabama—Chuck, Scott, Doug, and I managed to make the holiday visits to Arkansas regardless of distance.

On Thanksgiving Day 1995, we were gathered at my parents' home when one of those rare events happened that later makes you wish you could turn back the clock and do it over again. All four sisters, their spouses, and some of the grandchildren were there. Daddy was nearing the end of his life, and although still mobile at eighty-three, he had become quite frail.

As I was standing in the crowded living room getting ready to go to the dining room to eat the home-cooked meal we had prepared, I felt a presence beside me. Next, I felt someone brush against me and take my hand, gently squeezing it. Much to my dismay, I reacted in complete shock by jerking my hand away; only then did I realize it was Daddy who had taken my hand.

Why I reacted that way I can't say. For the first time in my life, he had tried to show me affection, and my first thought was to pull away and distance myself. Knowing all I had to do was squeeze his hand or put an arm around him could have been a tremendous step in the healing process for us both. I later realized Daddy was trying, in his own way, to tell me he loved me and was, perhaps, trying to show compassion.

Daddy passed away the next year at eighty-four, with the opportunity gone, never to come back.

On September 11, 2000, my beloved mother passed away at eighty-nine. Remarkably, she was still mentally sharp and well aware of her surroundings, but her body had finally betrayed her. Six months before she died, she broke her hip and never recovered. Mama was in a nursing home the last years of her life but never lost her sense of kindness and caring for others. Since I was single and living in Memphis, she was more concerned about me than she was about herself.

When Mama died, the nursing home staff made it a point to tell us how much they had loved her, what a special patient she had been, and how they would miss her. Expressions of sympathy poured in from all points as news of Mama's death became known. One of the most meaningful came from Mama's lifelong friend and fellow church member, Ethel Pettus. As her two sons were growing up in the New Castle Methodist Church, Mrs. Pettus asked them, "Who in the local New Castle community and church most exemplifies what you feel a Christian should be?" In response to her question, both responded, "Mrs. Mattie," that is, my mother.

After Mama's funeral service and burial, though we were divorced, Chuck walked up to me at the cemetery. With tears in both our eyes, he surprised me by saying: "Do something for me. You have spent your entire life doing for others—now do something for yourself." I was touched many times that day, but nothing touched me as deeply as his words.

I miss Mama and Daddy, but I'm grateful to have had parents who loved me. I loved Daddy, but Mama's death was harder. I have only good memories of the soft touch of her hands; though calloused and worn, they were ever so gentle. Ten years later, I still find myself having conversations with her.

Mama taught us many things, including the meaning of compassion and understanding. For us all, she modeled consistency, faithfulness, and endurance. She gave us wisdom and perspective. She made strong statements, not necessarily with words, but with her life. These are memories I will always carry with me and hope I can leave with my family as time marches on.

*Chapter 19*

♣

*9/11*

Shortly after my divorce in October 1999, I was delighted when FedEx Corporation responded to my employment application and extended an interview invitation. Although I had taken early retirement from TVA, I felt I could still make a contribution in my field of work. I was thrilled when I was offered the job and started work right away.

Working at the world headquarters of the world's largest express transportation company has been a great experience. Having recently been promoted, I am truly thankful for the opportunities offered me while at FedEx. I've grown both personally and professionally, and I attribute much of my growth to the amazing people with whom I've worked.

On September 10, 2001, Gene, my boss at FedEx, left Memphis en route to New York City on a company business trip. Accompanying him were his wife, Christine, and their eight-year-old daughter, Valerie. After arriving in New York and checking into the World Trade Center Hotel, Gene took his family to the top of the World Trade Center for a first-time visit. They took pictures and later, on a visit to Staten Island, took more pictures with the twin towers in the distance.

Gene, a highly respected member of FedEx Corporation's executive team, is known for his brilliant mind. Born and educated in China, he arrived in the United States in 1985 to continue postgraduate work at Yale University. After earning a master's degree at Yale, Gene earned his doctorate at the University of Pennsylvania.

Gene's wife, Christine, also a PhD, is professor of finance at the University of Memphis. Their daughter, Valerie, now a lovely teenager, is an award-winning pianist and harpist. An excellent student, she also finds time to perform with some of the top-rated symphony groups in the Memphis area.

A typical day in the office finds Gene and me planning

and arranging his business trips, meetings, and speeches. He travels throughout the world representing FedEx in his capacity as chief economist and vice president. He is a sought-after speaker and has appeared on CNN, CNBC, and other TV venues.

September 11, 2001, began like any other Tuesday morning as I arrived at the office and settled in at my desk. My thoughts were of my mother since that day was the one-year anniversary of her death, but those thoughts were replaced shortly with the happenings in New York City and elsewhere in the country.

As telephones began ringing with families and coworkers exchanging unbelievable news of the attacks, panic began to take hold as I realized Gene had a meeting scheduled that morning in the World Trade Center. Quickly checking his itinerary, I realized his meeting was in progress at the very moment the planes had struck the towers.

The staff and I immediately began trying to call him on his cell phone without success. Watching the events unfold on TV and knowing Gene's family was in the tower's hotel also, I prayed they would all get out alive, but it didn't look promising.

Gene rose early on the morning of September 11 to attend his 8:00 A.M. breakfast meeting in the South Tower. As he left the hotel room in the South Tower, Christine and Valerie told him they planned to have breakfast at the Windows on the World restaurant located on the top floor of the World Trade Center's North Tower..

During Gene's meeting, the attendees heard a loud explosion. The chandeliers shook, and security guards appeared in the meeting room and instructed the group to go to the lobby. Thinking it might have been a gas explosion, Gene called Christine and asked her to bring Valerie and meet him in the lobby. He was relieved to find that they were running a few minutes late and hadn't left their hotel room for the restaurant.

After Gene's call to Christine, she was hesitant to leave the room since the hotel staff was on the intercom urging guests to stay in their rooms. When Gene saw the smoke and debris falling outside the windows, his demeanor took on a sense of urgency, and he insisted his family vacate the room and come downstairs immediately.

Christine and Valerie rode the elevator to the lobby and met Gene. As they exited the South Tower, they saw that the smoke and debris had become very dense. As they looked upward, they were horrified to see the tail of a plane protruding from the North Tower of the World Trade Center. At that point they were unable to tell if it was a small plane or a large aircraft.

Seconds later the crowd heard the roaring engine of a low-flying aircraft directly overhead. Looking up, they saw a huge airliner, as if in slow motion, slam into the South Tower they had just vacated. The ground shook and people screamed, "Terrorist attack!" Some were shouting that an unmanned missile had struck its target.

As the North Tower and South Tower exploded and erupted in balls of fire, women dressed in business suits and men in white shirts and ties jumped from the windows. Gene saw as many as eighteen to twenty people jump and hit the pavement. He did his best to keep Valerie's eyes covered to block the scene.

As the buildings started to collapse, everyone ran, but they couldn't outrun the thick smoke and debris. As Gene held Christine and Valerie's hands, Valerie was separated from them and pushed to the ground by the crowd. A gentleman tried to help her up, but he too was knocked down by the crowd. Due to the thickness of the smoke, Gene and Christine lost sight of Valerie and began frantically calling her name. After what seemed like hours—but fortunately was only a few minutes—a lady brought Valerie to them and asked if she was their daughter. Valerie had lost her shoes but otherwise had only a few scrapes and bruises.

As they moved southwest with the crowd toward the Hudson River bank, one explosion after another occurred. People screamed and cried thinking Manhattan was under attack. Once the crowd got to the river, a weeping elderly lady told them not to jump in the river. They wanted to continue running but were hemmed in between the exploding towers behind them and the river in front of them.

Shortly afterward, police started arriving on the scene and asked them to move to the ferry station, where they were given wet cloths to cover their mouths to help them breathe. People were doing all they could to help each other.

The sky had begun to clear a little but was still dark with black smoke and debris as the group was ferried to Staten Island. Thinking they were now in the midst of a war, Gene was afraid the ferry would be torpedoed. Knowing neither his wife nor his daughter could swim, he asked himself, "If I can only save one of them, which will it be?" Fortunately, they arrived safely, and he didn't have to make that decision.

After the group arrived at Staten Island, family friends were eventually contacted to pick up Gene and his family. They had survived with only the clothes on their backs. All the personal possessions they had brought on their trip, including Gene's office laptop computer, which contained valuable company files and information were lost in the towers' destruction. Even so, they considered themselves extremely fortunate since the first plane hit the North Tower's Windows on the World restaurant, where Christine and Valerie would have been eating breakfast moments later. There were no survivors in the restaurant area.

As soon as he could get to a telephone, Gene called the office to let us know he was safe. The entire room broke into applause when I broke into a meeting to inform them of Gene's call.

# Chapter 20

♣

## Another Journey

A year after my divorce, in May 2001, I met another challenge: life handed me breast cancer.

There was no reason to fear the routine mammogram I had scheduled for that bright spring day. Having a history of benign cystic breast disease, it was not unusual for me to detect small lumps in my breasts. For this reason, an ultrasound was usually performed in addition to a mammogram during my yearly checkup.

Being called back to the X-ray room for additional slides was also normal. I thought nothing of it when the nurse called me back again and again for more pictures. After the doctor reviewed the final X-rays, the nurse told me I could get dressed. I thought, "This is great. The mammogram must have looked good, so there is no need for an ultrasound."

As I gathered my personal belongings to leave, the nurse walked over to me, and in a quiet voice said, "Mrs. Petty, the doctor needs to see you." It was at that moment that my life as I knew it changed.

As the doctor reviewed the X-rays with me, he said, "Mrs. Petty, you have some suspicious calcifications in your right breast. You need to see a surgeon right away." The office made an appointment with Dr. Martin Fleming, a well-known Memphis surgeon. Dr. Fleming performed a lumpectomy the following week.

The day of surgery, I arrived at the hospital at 6:00 A.M. to be "wired." After I questioned the medical staff about what being wired meant, the nurse said, "Oh, once that's over, the rest of the surgical procedure will be easier." Waiting for the wiring, I nervously flipped through a couple of magazines without really seeing anything on the pages.

A wire localization is a procedure that uses a mammogram to locate and identify breast abnormalities that can't be felt.

This helps the surgeon find the exact area to be removed and biopsied.

While I sat upright, my breast was positioned and compressed for a mammogram in order to find the location of the abnormal tissue. Once the area was identified, the radiologist administered a local anesthetic to numb my breast. The doctor inserted a large needle into my breast, and a small wire was threaded through the needle. Another mammogram was done to check correct placement of the wire. The doctor slowly withdrew the needle, leaving the localization wire in place. I felt very little pain during the procedure, only nausea from the pressure of the needle and the compression of the mammogram during the hour-long procedure.

After the wiring, I joined my family in the pre-op room where they were waiting. Shortly thereafter, I was wheeled to the operating room and given a general anesthetic.

The surgeon removed the area where the wire was located as well as the surrounding tissue. The tissue was sent to the breast imaging department to verify that the abnormality had been removed, and the specimen was then sent to pathology.

After I spent a couple of hours in the recovery room, the doctor discharged me. Before leaving the hospital, I made an appointment with the surgeon's office for the following week to get my results. Waiting for the results made for a long week, but I was optimistic since there was no history of breast cancer in my family and I had never been a smoker.

My sister, Marilyn, accompanied me to the doctor's office that Monday morning to get results of the lumpectomy. When the doctor walked into the treatment room accompanied by his nurse, I thought they had compassionate looks on their faces but quickly convinced myself that I had imagined this. Unfortunately, that was not the case. As kindly as he could, Dr. Fleming said, "The test results were positive for cancer. You can have either a mastectomy or seven weeks of radiation treatments." Initial pathology results indicated that the cancer had invaded the lymph nodes, but further tests showed this was not the case.

So, there I was on a journey—totally unprepared for what was happening to me. When I returned home from the doctor's office, I headed straight for the Internet to learn all I could; but as I tried to read, the words just ran together, and I was unable to focus. Thoughts ran through my head of all the things I should have done or could have done to prevent the cancer. Had I not eaten enough fresh fruits and vegetables? Had I not exercised enough? Should I not have taken hormone replacement therapy since my hysterectomy in 1983?

Deciding whether to have a mastectomy or radiation treatments was not an easy choice to make. In the end I decided on the radiation treatments based on two factors: One, since there was no history of breast cancer in my family, I thought this was likely a one-time occurrence. Two, since chemotherapy hadn't been recommended, I felt the cancer treatments would be less severe than if the cancer had invaded the lymph nodes.

A lymph node, also called a lymph gland, consists of lymphatic tissue surrounded by a capsule of connective tissue. Lymph nodes are part of the lymphatic system, which is part of the body's immune system. Lymph nodes can play a role in breast cancer, as the lymphatic system can move cancer cells throughout the body. Cancer can spread through the body either through the bloodstream or through the lymph nodes. I felt extremely fortunate that my cancer had not spread beyond my breast.

A round of visits to a radiation oncologist followed, and plans were set in place to begin the first of thirty-four radiation treatments. Support from family, friends, and co-workers sustained me through the rigorous process. My boss was tremendous, giving me wide flexibility in my work schedule. By the third week of treatments, when I was losing weight and becoming weak with increasing fatigue, my boss encouraged me to shorten my workday in order to get rest and conserve my strength. I was able to complete the full course of treatments without missing a full day of work.

As I regained strength and my body started to heal, so did my mind. It became clear to me what was truly important, which allowed me to let go of the negative parts of my life and move forward. After the cancer diagnosis, I developed a deeper appreciation for family and friends. Although I had always loved my family, I finally realized they were the most important part of my life.

For the next six years, I held my breath with every mammogram and ultrasound, hoping remission would be permanent. However, in 2007, cancer made its re-entry into my life with a malignancy in my left breast. This time, knowing what to expect, I found the news even more daunting.

The second lumpectomy was performed with the same positive results as before; however, treatment would be different this time. After consulting with my surgeon, who referred me to an oncologist, who referred me to a radiation oncologist, the decision was made to treat the cancer with oral chemotherapy and monitor my progress with a mammogram every six months.

There are many "what ifs" that creep into my mind every day. What if the cancer returns? What if the pain in my back, arm, or leg is cancer? But it is comforting to be told that most of what scares us turns out to be nothing—and that most women with breast cancer go on to live fuller, richer lives than they thought possible.

I lived through what many women fear more than anything else—a diagnosis of breast cancer. Strength acquired over a lifetime of challenges again taught me to make the best of a tough situation.

I've found I'm a much stronger person than I ever gave myself credit for being. In many ways, having cancer has enriched my life and made me recognize that every day is a gift—which is why it's called the present. It is my hope and prayer that a cure for cancer will be found in my lifetime. As of now, the cancer is again in remission.

*Chapter 21*

♣

*Happiness*

*Being happy doesn't mean everything's perfect. It means you've decided to see beyond the imperfections.*

In September 1999 I happened to run into John again. After I told him of my pending divorce, we exchanged phone numbers, and I hoped John would call. He still lived in Nashville, and I was living in Memphis. John did call, and after my divorce was final, we began seeing each other and continued to do so for several years.

Having much in common was part of what attracted us to each other. Also, developing a friendship in earlier years and gradually getting to know each other deepened our feelings and suggested an old-fashioned love first developed by friendship.

John and I shared many happy times, taking short trips and just being together. I came to know his family, and we took vacations together. He not only became my dearest friend but also the one true love every woman hopes to find. We discussed marriage but both felt we were comfortable as things were. We are still friends and keep in touch, but due to health issues that prevent John from traveling on his own, we no longer see each other. He, too, will always have a special place in my heart.

❧

As many people will attest, the birth of grandchildren is one of life's richest blessings, and the same has been true for me. Though my two sons are the greatest gift I have ever received, grandchildren have brought immeasurable joy into my life. They are precious treasures who will always be a special part of me.

After our two sons were born, I thought briefly about

having another child, perhaps even through adoption. I dreamed of some day having a daughter in addition to the two boys. After much consideration, I decided to wait for grandchildren—perhaps a granddaughter.

When Scott and his wife Ceilia announced she was pregnant, I secretly hoped for a girl. To my delight, they had *twin* girls. Our beautiful identical-twin granddaughters, Riley Kathryn and Caley Ann, were born January 1996. I loved buying matching outfits and dressing them when they were small. Since they live nearby, I am involved in their lives and school activities. They are now cheerleaders on their high school team and will be competing in national competition next spring.

Nineteen months after the twins were born, our third grandchild, Hunter, was born to Scott and Ceilia. It was a busy time with all three kids in diapers at the same time. Hunter, now a handsome young man, is especially close to his father. Being a dedicated sports fan, Scott delights in taking his son to sporting events like home and out-of-town University of Memphis football and basketball games.

❧

In 2005 I contracted to have a condo built in a lovely upscale area near Memphis called Collierville. Since the house I owned at the time sold immediately, I lived with my son Doug while the condo was under construction.

While living with Doug, I became acquainted with Vince and Barb, two of his neighbors, who were active in the Memphis Bop Club. They invited me to go dancing with them one Friday night, but I wasn't interested since I had never felt comfortable on the dance floor. I finally decided to go only because they kept encouraging me to do so.

I danced a few times during the night, all the while

watching the clock, waiting for the night to end and thinking this one time would be it. The next week, I hoped Barb wouldn't ask, but she did. For some reason I said yes and didn't feel quite as intimidated at the dance as I had the first week. The dancers at the club were very friendly and made me feel welcome.

The third week, as we sat watching the other dancers, an attractive gentleman came over and asked Vince and Barb to introduce us. His name was Louis (Lou for short). Lou had a nice build, wavy hair, and bright blue eyes. He asked me to dance, and after I went through my usual spiel of telling him I wasn't a good dancer, he said, "Well, we will teach you." He was very patient and spent a lot of time showing me some basic dance steps.

Feeling emotionally handicapped due to having been somewhat battered by life and love, I was afraid to put my trust in Lou, but I discovered that sometimes you just have to find a person who—despite your faults—still thinks you are the perfect dance partner.

Lou and I started dating, and we continue to see each other. Lou is a retired college professor with a love of horses. He has a fifty-acre farm with a large house, barn, horses, and a lake. Though we have no long-term plans, he has been a welcome part of my life for the past four years. A kind and considerate person, he recently gave me a card on which he had written, "You have more good qualities than anyone I have ever met."

When I met Lou, I had reached a point in my life where I felt that the relationship I had hoped for was not going to happen, so I concentrated on making the best life for myself that I could. I planned and built my home in Collierville to be near my sons and grandchildren where I felt I would have things the way I wanted them. Then Lou showed up. So now

I am doing my best to open doors I had closed and to make a special place in my life and my heart for him.

❧

I have made plenty of mistakes during my lifetime, but today I can face life with a new sense of purpose. Each of us just has to turn that page and go on to the next one. I know I must accept responsibility for my own mistakes. Realizing that it is not all about me and knowing what it means to love, to be loved, to hurt, to need someone to understand me—and, finally, to feel that I belong and am accepted as I am—are all lessons I have learned on life's pathway.

I have been told that I'm a person whose mind is very compartmentalized, unlike those free spirits whose minds are like open plains with no restrictions and no real focus. My mind is usually focused on whatever compartment is on the block at the time. When that block has been taken care of, I go to the next one, constantly focused and constantly taking care of business.

I developed this method of dealing with life because from early childhood and on into adulthood, the burden of what was expected of me knew no end; there was always work to be done. The luxury of procrastinating was never an option. I believe I was motivated by a burning desire to do better for myself and others.

As each year passes, I have become more and more content with who I am and how I have lived my life. I am constantly reminded of how precious each day of life is and how important it is to enjoy every step along the way.

❧

Sometimes life hands us unexpected blessings. Over

time, life has handed me the gift of forgiveness. Forgiveness really is a gift for all of us; it gives us the freedom to move forward. Archbishop Desmond Tutu says, "Forgiveness is the grace by which you enable the other person to get up, and get up with dignity, to begin anew."

With a new awareness of how strongly I was harboring bitterness and resentment over some past hurts and old wounds associated with my marriage and divorce, I came to the realization that I could either forgive or continue to feel I was the victim. For me to go on and not live with anger and resentment every day of my life, I had to forgive. Staying angry was not an option.

I found that forgiveness is, first of all, a journey. Beginning on the forgiveness journey involved recognizing my own thoughts, feelings, and pain. I found that genuine forgiveness takes time and courage. I was challenged to give up negative thoughts about situations in my life and believe in the possibility of a brighter future.

Coming to appreciate the love, beauty, and kindness around me, I realized that forgiveness and compassion are necessary for true happiness. I've learned that in order to have compassion for others, I must first have compassion for myself. Continuing to hold on to the past, regardless of the situation, is a deterrent to happiness.

Forgiving Chuck, as well as myself, for mistakes in our marriage and divorce has been a healing process. I am very much aware that as Chuck became older he came to admire me for who the timid country girl he married had grown into. I also believe he was proud of me, although he was never able to say so to me. Most of all, I know Chuck loved me—and for this gift I am grateful.

{~}

While doing research for this book, I discovered a delightful blog, called the "Peach Fuzz Chronicles," created by some of my former high school classmates. Memories recalled by the bloggers introduced me to a whole new world. While this world had existed around me while I grew up and attended school, I was oblivious to its presence. The normal lives these bloggers had experienced as teenagers, growing up in our small town and participating in what the city and school had to offer, read like a novel to me. Bloggers shared memories of spending long summer days at the Forrest City public swimming pool, going to the Skipper for hamburgers and Cokes on Friday or Saturday nights, and going to the Corral after football games to dance to the latest songs on the jukebox.

The Forrest City High School fraternities and sororities actually rented buses and attended formals in Memphis. There was the traditional Thanksgiving Day football game between Forrest City and nearby Wynne, where the girls' dates bought mum corsages for them to wear on their mouton coats.

As one blogger writes, "Forrest City was a great place to come of age. I talk about growing up there to people everywhere." Another blogger says, "It is that mystery bond of a childhood in Forrest City that not only does not go away, but grows in strength with the years and encompasses all of us from around the world in all walks of life. Yes, this blog makes us realize what a precious gift we had of living in Forrest City as children. We laugh about the bad things but you know what? It was the bad things that prepared us for life. I think the town taught us well."

༄

Attending high school reunions over the years and

connecting with many of my former schoolmates has been a catharsis. We all have pains from the past, but as we age we sometimes lose sight of how all the things that happened to us along our journey had a purpose. It is important to be able to reach back in time, making good memories as well as bad ones come to mind, and realize that each failure, success, tear, laugh, and thought—basically every emotion we had—made the mold for the person we are today.

Receiving an invitation to attend my ten-year high school reunion, I wondered, "Why would I want to remember those years and go through that again?" Personally, I couldn't wait to escape the farm *and* the town and be somebody besides that gawky girl in my graduation picture. Yet, strangely enough, I was one of those eager faces that showed up. At the time, Chuck and I were married and living in Memphis with our two small sons.

So, why did I—and the other hundred or so others—go back? Reuniting with former classmates, I met some wearing nametags, which were certainly needed, and we swapped stories about our children and careers. We took pictures and whispered about who had gone to prison and for what, while displaying our pride in the doctors, lawyers, ministers, and others whose accomplishments made us proud.

Amid all the greetings and laughter, a beautiful thing happened: cliques vanished as we found ourselves wishing we had known each other better. One central theme among people I talked to was how little we actually knew back then—and I had thought I was the only one who was naive and didn't have a clue.

Lining up for a professional class photograph, I overheard one of my former popular male classmates comment to one of his friends in the back row, "Who is the girl in the white dress on the front row? How did we miss that?" Since I was the only one on the front row in a white dress, I smiled as

I thought about how time changes the way we see others. Perhaps they no longer saw me as the sharecropper's daughter or the poor farm girl.

Writer John Grady remarked, "Reunions change reality. The 10-year reunion is about impressing your former peers—showing them, and perhaps yourself, that you made it. By the 20th reunion, you get to just be yourself."

At our fiftieth reunion, names of the twenty-seven classmates who had passed away were read as a bell tolled for each. We didn't cry. Instead our emotions came out in hugs—hugs from people we had learned to treasure more than we had before. There was the hug from a male classmate not remembered but who said he would know you anywhere; hugs from farmers, professors, old boyfriends. The hugs told us, "You're still here."

Driving back home to Memphis that night, I felt fulfilled—glad I had gone but gladder to be returning home. After leaving the reunion site at Forrest City Country Club, I drove by and took one last look at the massive two-story, red brick schoolhouse. Just one last glance and then it was gone.

ꙮ

Looking back at the circumstances that were most influential in shaping my life, it's clear the ones that tested me the most were also the ones that caused me to grow the most. Experiencing those times, I never considered that they were teaching me humbleness, endurance, commitment, empathy, or ethics, as they certainly were—and even directing me toward the eventual life paths I would choose and further learn from.

As the years progress, amazingly I am becoming more and more thankful for each of those events, and I am reminded of these loving words of promise from the Bible, "I know the plans I have for you, declares the Lord, plans to prosper you and not to harm you, plans to give you hope and a future." (Jeremiah 29:11)

**Mama's first plane ride**

**Mama crowned queen of Wynwood Nursing Home**

**Daddy and his long awaited tractor**

**Daddy in later years**

**Glenda, Marilyn, Clara, Bill, and Maxine**

**Doug**

Doug on the golf course

**Scott**

**Hunter, Scott, Caley, and Riley on
Caribbean cruise, 2009**

**Hunter and Clara**

**Riley and Caley**

Twins – Riley and Caley

**Lou, Clara, Marilyn, and Don**

**Doug, Hunter, Caley, Clara, Riley, and Scott on our Caribbean cruise, 2010**

References

1. Child Labor Standards Act: An Overview of Federal Child Labor Laws, http://www.ourownbackyard.com, p.1

2. Ibid., p.4

3. Press Release, CARE ACT Would Protect 500,000 Child Farmworkers, www.stopchildlabor.org/pressroom/061207_care_act.html, p.1

4. Ibid., p.2

5. The Hidden Problem of Child Farmworkers in America, Summary of a Human Rights Watch Report on Child Labor in the U.S., Source *Fingers to the Bone.* U.S. Failure to Protect Child Farmworkers, Human Rights Watch, 22000, p.1

6. Ibid., p.2

7. Ibid., p.3

8. Ibid., p.4

9. Wikipedia, the free encyclopedia, http://en.wikipedia.org.wiki/Forrest_City_Arkansas, p.1

10. Ibid., p.2

11. Ibid., p.3

12. Crime Library, Criminal Minds and Methods, http://www.crimelibrary.com/criminal_mind/sexual_assualt/severed_penis/7.html, p.1

13. Harkavy, Ward, The Castration of Wayne Dumond, A Pardon That Clinton Didn't Grant, 3/6/01, http://www.villagevoice.com/news/0110,harkavy,22841,1html, p.1

14. Breast Wire Localization Biopsy, www.cancermed.umich.edu/prevention/breast_wire_localization_biopsy.shtml,p.1

15. Ibid., p.2
16. Ibid., p.3
17. UCSF Medical Center, Needles (wire) Localization Biopsy, http://www.ucsfhealth. org/adult/medical_services/cancer/breast, needle biopsy.html, p.1
18. Author unknown
19. *Covington Leader*, 1/20/93, Section B, p.1
20. *Memphis Press Scimitar*, 12/10/77, p.10
21. *The Elaine Riot: Tragedy & Triumph, Teacher's Guide*, funded by Winthrop Rockefeller Foundation, p. 2.
22. Ibid., p.3
23. Ibid., p.4
24. Ibid., p.5
25. Ibid., p.6
26. *Times Herald*, Forrest City, Arkansas, 12/20/89, p.6.
27. 27. "The Real Causes of Two Race Riots," http:// www.yale.edu/glc/archive/1136.htm, p.3
28. Ibid., p.4
29. Ibid., p.5
30. Ibid., p.6
31. Ibid., p.7
32. 32."Elaine Race Riot," Wikipedia, the free encyclopedia, http://en.wikipedia.org/wiki/ Elaine_Race_Riot, p. 2
33. Whitaker, Robert, *On the Laps of Gods, The Red Summer of 1919 and the Struggle for Justice That Remade a Nation*, p.99
34. Ibid., p.109
35. Ibid., p.112
36. Ibid., p.100
37. Ibid., p.117

38. Ibid., p.118
39. Ibid., p.124
40. Ibid., p.125
41. Ibid., p.126
42. Ibid., p.127
43. Ibid., p.128
44. Ibid., p.132
45. Ibid., p.135
46. Ibid., p.160
47. Ibid., p.162
48. Ibid., p.163
49. Ibid., p.164
50. Wells Barnett, Ida B., *The Arkansas Race Riot*, 1920, pg.1
51. Wikipedia, the free encyclopedia, pg.80, 81
52. Hennacy, Ammon, Catholic Worker home page, pg.19
53. Lambert, Gerald, *All Out of Step*

LaVergne, TN USA
09 November 2010
204203LV00001B/4/P